Preface

Welsh Collie Bramble lived to 25 years old an[d was] the worlds oldest bitch. This book documents [her] diet. It demonstrates how to circumvent the pe[t food industry that] contributes to greenhouse gasses and Animal [suffering]. It is also the story of the humans who cared for Bramble, and working class lives and struggles in Somerset from the 1950's to the present day.

It encapsulates a philosophy on how to facilitate longevity in the animals that live with us, whilst bringing you snap shots of the lives of people like my ex soldier and trade unionist father, whose efforts on behalf of his colleagues enabled working class voices to be heard across the century.

It is a memoir of a bolshy welsh dog and the voices of Somerset folk. The ones you don't usually hear.
The book has a non-linear narrative so chapters can be read in any order.

Dedicated with love and gratitude to my Grandmother Edith May Rawle, and Dogs; Bramble, Floyd, sally, Stan, Squeak, and Dreadlock. Being with you was amazing. You're all gone but never forgotten, as if anyone could.

Contents

Chapter one.   Floyd the vegan dog. P.3

Chapter two.   Bramble the dog from Wales. P.17

Chapter three. Bramble speaks; Listening to dogs. P.27

Chapter four.   Vets; Negotiating a health plan. P.37

Chapter five.   Floyd dies. P.47

Chapter six.   Bramble has an accident. P.59

Chapter seven. Respecting dogs. P.68

Chapter eight.   Caring for elderly creatures. P.81

Chapter nine.   Bramble dies. P.91

Chapter One

Floyd, the Vegan Dog.

Somerset in the nineteen fifties was a good place to be born. My family home was a terraced council house that stood on the edge of acres of meadow. My first memory is of looking out of my front facing bedroom window onto the fields of bright yellow buttercups. Across from our house was a tree that was home to a little owl that mum says used to hoot throughout the night. In front of our garden was a small road and then the fields fringed with hedges of hawthorn, blackthorn and brambles. In the autumn the estate children spent hours picking the blackberries that grew in the hedges. We sold them to housewives or shops for a few pennies, then went home covered in purple stains with torn dresses and scratched hands.

To get into the fields children dug holes under the wire fence that surrounded the hedgerows but it was still a scramble to get through the prickly hedge. Spikes of blackthorn pierced our clothes and painfully caught our hair. The struggle through the hedge was worth it. Once inside the fields there was another kingdom away from the concrete council estate with its wide grey pavements and identical homes.

Seasonally the fields were awash with colour from wave upon wave of wild flowers. As well as an ocean of buttercups there were tall mauve cuckoo pint flowers growing in the boggy soil and there was a little orchard that filled with fragrant cowslips in the spring. I would bend down to smell the scented flowers in the orchards tall damp grass.

Most of the time local children were allowed out to roam the fields away from the busy life of the estate. On Sundays I would take a packed lunch of sandwiches, fruit and orange juice and put it in my school satchel. Then it was possible with parental permission, to stay out in the fields all day. Sometimes with a school friend I would attempt to walk to Cheddar. We never got there across the miles of fields but we would straddle the fences and jump over ditches that in those days were full of stickleback fish and newts. There was a derelict farmhouse on the edge of the fields and its garden was full of wild strawberries that we stopped to pick and eat. We pretended to be spies or private detectives as we walked depending on what we had watched on our parents new Sobel televisions.

Alongside the fields ran two lanes, Bower and Dunwear. Mum said that Bower Lane had been marched along by the Duke of Monmouth and his peasant army in 1685. They met their deaths at nearby Westonzoyland while trying to claim the crown from the King. Dunwear was mums favourite. Apple orchards lined the roads back then. The trees were standard size and covered in pink and green fruit which looked like they might have been drawn by the hands of children. There was a shop along the lane where sweets and orange ice lollies could be bought, and there was a house where the outside wall was clad in shells and shiny pebbles. Further along the lane horses grazed and just after that you could walk along the river. While my brother and I walked beside our mother Nancy, she would tell us about things we could do with our lives. One idea which seemed to be her favourite involved buying a big removal van kitted out with beds and hot water and driving away in it. Far past the council estate. Mum never mentioned who would pay for diesel or food but it remained an exciting possibility in our minds. When we were out shopping she would pick up things in stores like Woolworths or Timothy Whites and say " This would be useful for when we move into the lorry".

Before we were old enough for school our lives centred on the house, number forty three Moorland road. It was big and airy with windows at both ends of the sitting room. Sometimes moates of light cast rainbows onto the walls and mum said these could be fairies and that we should run and try to catch them. The back garden was huge. Dad sectioned it off to lawn, a vegetable patch and play area. He built a black picket fence around it on which he trained roses and put up a metal swing. As well as working twelve hour days at the post office supplies in Bridgwaters Bristol road, dad was secretary of the post office engineering union and still found time to grow many of our vegetables. The back garden was kept neat with rows of onions, cabbage, potatoes and fruit. Dad never learned to drive and rode his bicycle everywhere. Mum, David and I walked or caught the bus. The Sydenham estate was far away from the other end of town that was home to our Grandparents. On free days we would walk a few miles each way to their houses.

Maternal grandmother Grace lived with Grandfather Hubert. He liked to read about the ancient Britons, draw celtic patterns and hide in his shed. Grace was more of a people person, and an avid gardener. Her patch at the back of the house was always filled with the scent of flowers. A large pink camellia was planted by the back window and behind that were rows of rannuncula, pansies and London pride, with annuals and perrinials planted as far along as Huberts vegetable patch. Grace had many adult friends and at Christmas and holidays we were welcome in the house. Mum said at other times Grace wasn't wild about children. It was to parental grandmother Edith May Heritage, nee Rawles house that we walked most often. Grandad Harold Heritage was chairman of the North ward labour party and politics dominated his conversation day and night. Edith was interested too but she doted on her grandchildren. On Saturdays I visited her on my own to luxuriate in her grandmotherly care. She kept a coal fire burning in the hearth and the flames that licked the logs were reflected in the brass fire fender. Up to this she would push the big settee and I would be invited to lie upon it. Gran would then wait on me with cakes, comics and other treats that were harder to come by at home. At Moorland road David seemed to be mums favourite. I felt this was apparent in our differing care. Although younger he went to bed later at night. Sometimes I was smacked. That would never happen to David.
I had a recurring dream of abandonment. Mum and David would drive past me in a bus. In the dream mum would say " We'll meet again one day".

Between mum and I food was a bone of contention. Money was short because Dad was saving the deposit to buy a house. On Davids bedroom wall mum had pasted pictures of shop bought cakes we couldn't afford, cut from magazines. Food waste was not tolerated. If I couldn't eat my dinner it took on the proportions of a tragedy. Mums housekeeping money only allowed for cheap meat. Dad ate offal, faggots, tripe and chittling. He ate it cheerily with pickle. I couldn't stomach meat. Mum cooked pale sausages that were burnt outside and raw in the middle. I couldn't swallow them without huge gulps of water. Whilst Nancys baking was wonderful with chocolate or coffee cakes and raspberry buns, her boiled veg was watery and the potatoes made me retch. I was smacked once or twice for wasting an inedible dinner. Gran didn't bake so much but her potatoes were creamy and vegetables well cooked. If I couldn't eat all her dinners it was never any problem.

Mum liked to read ghost stories. One was about a haunting where the ghost of a nanny came back to kill real children. Her favourite book was a poltergeist tale about a haunting at a building called Borely Rectory. These ghost stories frightened me and I felt safer at Grans house than at home.

One lunch time when David and I were about to eat cornish pasty and chips, our aunt Dinah came to visit. Something seemed wrong about this. She rarely visited at midday. As we started to eat mum said conversationally "Your granny Heritage is dead". Everything seemed to slow down. I looked at my brother who had paused with his fork in the air. My aunt was looking at me waiting for a reaction. This did not seem possible.

"You're a liar" I spat at my waiting mother. I fled from the room and ran down the road. Tears streamed from my eyes as I pounded along the pavement. There would be no more comics by the open fire. No more cuddles or gentle encouragement. No more magical days alone with Granny. From now on it would be me being the odd one out. Ghostly stranglings and Borely Rectory. David being the golden boy at home and me alone. These were my thoughts as I ran to my cousins house. Granny had died from a stroke. We were not allowed to see her body although I asked. Instead mum said I could give a ring to be put on grannys finger in the coffin. I chose a square silver ring with a clear stone that I always wore and handed it to mum. She said she would pass it to grandad to do the honours. From that moment I became the outsider in the family. The child without a champion

Mum was always too busy to have friends. This meant that David and I did not have many either. Instead whilst running around outside I was befriended by the local dogs. In the sixties traffic was less and not everyone walked their dogs formally. Many people put them out of the house to wander around alone. These animals became my company. We would sit around in the sun together and if the older local boys tried to bully me my canine companions would run after them and nip at their heels. It would be wonderful to have a dog at home. She could be an ally in the house. I asked mum to ask dad if we could have one. The answer was a resounding no. Many years later I found out that when dad was a boy his mothers dog had been shot by a farmer and it had caused much upset in the house. This memory may have been a factor in his refusal. Dads word was law though, so there would be no dog in the house. No cats either. They would cost too much to feed. We were allowed other animals. Mum bought a hamster, tortoise and rabbit. One by one these animals died. Mum had put the hamster in a hutch in the garden where it died of cold. The hibernation of the tortoise failed and her shell filled up with maggots. My father put wire wool instead of bedding in the rabbits cage and he ate the wool and died. As a child I didn't understand why my pets were dying. It instilled in me though a desire to treat all animals kindly. With gentleness, respect and infinite care. In the meantime until I left home these were the years without a dog.

By the time I brought my first dog home I was in my late teens. My parents had moved from the council estate and bought a home at the other end of town. Dads mum hadn't lived to see this but they bought a house near to Harold. I left home at sixteen and went to work in a hotel in London but quickly decided that the city was not for me. Returning to the beautiful lanes and countryside of Somerset I bought a share in a house with a work collegue. The co-owner of my home was willing to accommodate a dog in the house. He also agreed to pay half of all the vets bills and dog food. A happy situation indeed. In the intervening years between childhood and buying a home I had become Vegan. The concept had been introduced to me by two women who had published some of my poetry in a journal they edited. In those days commercial vegan food was hard to find. At the time I was on a strict budget with a low paid job. I started to read books about nutrition and ecology. My mother was an avid reader of health books and she recommended some to me. I began to evolve a vegan diet. To keep costs down I bought in bulk and kept things simple. The main meal of the day became a dish of legumes, soya protein and vegetables. It had brown rice in it to supply fibre, vitamins B2 and B6. Yeast extract for B12, lentils for protein and vegetables for further vitamins and minerals. It was cooked from scratch every day. Thrown in a pan of water and left to simmer for an hour. It was more chemistry than recipe but it supplied nutrition at minimal cost. By now I was reading about animal rights and didn't want cows to be killed to feed my dog. I decided that the new canine addition to the house would be vegan. I had never heard of dogs being fed a vegan diet but I had done my research and knew many animals could thrive on food without animal products. Dogs and humans both being mammals I believed my new dog could thrive without meat. With this in mind my workmate and I stocked up on rice, textured vegetable protein and legumes then went to find a dog to rehome.

Our first attempt to become dog carers was unsuccessful. We took a taxi to the local animal shelter but it was closed due to parvo virus. Disconsolate that my first attempt to adopt had been thwarted I moaned at length to the taxi driver. It turned out he had two collie cross bitches who were half sisters that he was trying to rehome. He drove us to a large council estate on the edge of a neighbouring town. At the door he was greeted by his wife and child. The woman was pregnant again and so wanted to rehome her dogs. As she spoke to us two young collie cross bitches ran through her door out into the front garden. They were both eighteen months old and black and white. Phoebe had lots of border collie in her breeding and sported a large white ruff. Her half sister Floyd was a collie crossed with spaniel and she came over to Chris and I to say hello. She stood in front of me and looked up into my face with solemn dark brown eyes. Then she went over to the taxi driver who had picked up her blue lead. Phoebe didn't come over to us but stayed near her female owner. When both dogs had their leads on we walked around the block with them so we could decide which one to adopt. They were both charming and well mannered and we couldn't decide between them. "why don't you take them both home?" suggested the taxi driver. Chris and I did a quick calculation about the cost of extra food and finding we could afford to feed both dogs we took them home on the bus.

Home at this time was a small two bedroom terraced house on the way out of town. It had little gardens back and front with a lane at the rear backing onto an estate. There was no deposit needed for its purchase because the mortgage was one hundred per cent. It was the first time I'd had my own garden. Having watched my grandparents and father growing food I couldn't wait to get started myself. The back garden was laid to lawn with a couple of rose bushes, a passion flower and a shed at the end of a path. I started to read books about herbs and herbal medicine. Chris dug up the lawn so I could plant fruit and veg. The bottom of the garden I kept for herbs. A local health food store sold them grown in pots. For a month I bought new herbs every day and planted them in the garden. one of my favourites was mint, I planted pepper, pineapple, ginger mint and more. I began to use these fresh organic herbs in my cooking everyday. A handful of chopped mint was often thrown into the dogs dinner.

The dogs and I ate the same thing every day. By now the rice meal had become our staple diet. This was whole, long grain brown rice, red split lentils, textured vegetable protein, yeast extract, mint, tumeric and organic vegetables. Many of which I grew in the garden. With more reading I learnt about soil types, plants, their diseases and pests. I planted dwarf fruit trees of apples, plums and pears. Thus on a limited income with some labour I managed to feed myself and two dogs without great expense.

Floyd and Phoebe were a pleasure to care for. Both were bright, intelligent dogs with a mischevious sense of humour. Phoebe received much attention when out walking. She gravitated towards people and basked in their admiration. Floyd was more reserved and hung back behind her sister. Truth told Floyd couldn't be bothered with people. For whatever reason she wasn't interested in humans. The exception being me. While Chris spent time walking both of them more often he would end up playing ball with Phoebe who liked to keep him out of trouble. Floyd would be off sniffing cow pats and other ghastly things in the fields. While beautiful Phoebe would fetch the ball and return home pristine white, Floyd would trail home from walks covered in cow dung, dead fish or slime from a swim in the pond. Worse she liked to urinate in the house, often on the carpets. It seemed to us over a period of time that Floyd felt eclipsed by Phoebe, the dog who attracted so much outdoor attention . We felt that Floyd was unhappy and we came to a decision to split them up. We had discovered that the reason the taxi driver had given the dogs away was that he knew Floyd was pregnant. He hadn't bothered to say. We thought that no one would take on a pregnant dog so it was Floyd we kept and Phoebe we rehomed. Phoebe went to live with an elderly lady who wanted a companion for her existing dog. She had met Phoebe while we were walking with her and she lived by the river. She seemed kind and sensible and was happy to take Phoebe on.

With no one to compete with Floyd became more comfortable at home. She had given birth to four puppies just before Phoebe left and her puppies were large and strong. They were born one evening after a walk with Chris in the fields. Half way through her usual walking time Floyd took the lead in her mouth and guided Chris back home. Soon after she lay in her favourite place at home and her labour started. In a few hours she had produced four beautiful puppies, two bitches and two dogs. They were mainly black with little white bibs and paws. The biggest puppy was a bitch we called Castro. She grew quickly and liked to boss her mum. The smallest we called Che. He was sweet and gentle, fond of falling asleep on my lap.

One evening a knock on the door alerted us to the fact that Floyd had been run over. She had been safely ensconced in the back garden which was fenced all around and had a six foot high gate. A neighbour had seen her climb the gate like a cat and take herself out for an extra walk. She had only been out briefly when a car hit her at the end of our road. She crawled home with a fractured pelvis and could no longer feed her pups. We called the vet who came straight away. He attended to Floyd and gave us formula to feed the puppies. The pups lived with us for a few more weeks. We took them to Floyd one at a time because they were boisterous and she needed time to heal. Eventually we found homes for them. People asked us what we fed their mum on as they were the biggest puppies for their age that their new carers had ever seen. It was sad to let them go. By then Floyd and I were the best of friends. The house was small and so were my finances so they were better off rehomed, but many years later when beautiful Floyd had died I wished I had kept at least one of her offspring.

Floyd and I were close. One afternoon she saved my life. We were taking our usual walk in the fields near the house. It was towards evening and the sun had begun to set over the resovoir . The farmer who owned the fields kept cows there and didn't use much pesticide. In the spring and summer the meadows held a profusion of flowers. Walking through the yellow and pink carpet of buttercups, clover and cuckoo pint in the dusk I decided to take a short cut to another field by jumping over a deep but narrow rhyne. I called to Floyd to do the same but she was reluctant. Taking a run at the ditch I tried to launch myself over it but instead or reaching the far side bank I landed in the water. It was freezing cold and the rhyne seemed to have no bottom. One of my boots came off as I struggled to grab the vegetation at the edge of the ditch. The plants just broke off in my hand. There was nothing I could use as a lever to haul myself up onto the bank. A fleeting thought of drowning crossed my mind but suddenly Floyd was there. She came to the edge of the rhyne bracing her shoulders and staying near me so I could grab her ruff just long enough to give myself a hold to get up onto the bank. I pulled myself out of the water and retrieved my boot. Once she saw I was safe Floyd became furious with me. She grabbed my wringing wet sleeve and marched me home via the most direct route she could find through the remaining fields. She refused to let go of my sleeve until we were back in the house with the front door shut. Clearly she thought I was incapable of looking after myself.

This was my first glimpse of what I used to think of as her superior intelligence. I decided to teach her lots of human words to make the most of our communication. I taught her all the names of her toys and the vegetables I put in her dinner. I would hold things up " Look Floyd it's your bouncy ball" or "It's a carrot for your dinner". I had read about someone who had tried to teach a monkey complex language. The monkey was a mother with a baby. Although the mother wasn't that interested in what the human had to say the baby monkey started to learn human words. I knew it was possible for verbal communication to be understood between species so I spent hours talking to Floyd about everything and anything. At one time I was very interested in my garden. One afternoon having decided to plant seeds I thought Floyd might like to help me. Kneeling down putting runner bean seeds in a trench I couldn't reach the trowel. "Floyd will you help me, the trowels on the path, can you fetch it here?". Floyd seized upon the trowel, ran over to me and dropped it in the bean trench. I gave her a big cuddle. "well done sweetie, you're such a clever girl" Floyd loved to join in. Fetching small packets of seeds or the trowel became the gardening game. One night after we had been planting broad bean seeds I went to her basket to pick up her blanket to wash. There underneath it all around the edge of her basket was a curved arc of broad bean seeds. It looked like Floyd had decided to branch out and grow some beans of her own.

I loved that dog so much. We became an inseperable team. Each day we spent hours in the fields, at the crack of dawn, midday and dusk. First light we would be up and crossing the estate to disappear into the meadows.

11

Floyd never pulled on her lead but walked like a compressed spring, always full of excitement. At the time it was possible to walk some distance in the Hamp fields. The first meadow was full of cows and their excreta which I negotiated carefully. Floyd liked to roll in it and cover her ears in dung. Most days she would find an evil smell to roll in and I would have to say "Don't come too close. You stink you dirty devil". Dead fish were her other favourite especially if she had been required to have a bath. She clearly preferred the stink of rotting fish corpse to the smell of baths and shampoo. The Hamp fields were often covered in water and flooded to a depth of about six inches in winter, Floyd especially loved walking in them then. I followed along in thick socks and wellington boots. It was possible to walk some distance without much human company, just lots of birds, badgers, foxes and other wildlife. Floyd was such a well behaved and clever dog. We were having a wonderful time. I decided to rescue another dog as a companion for Floyd, because I believed
that caring for dogs was so easy.

My first outing with dad.

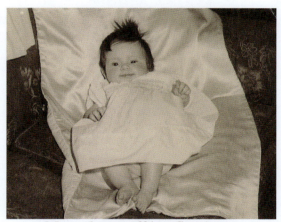

Mum shows off her first born.

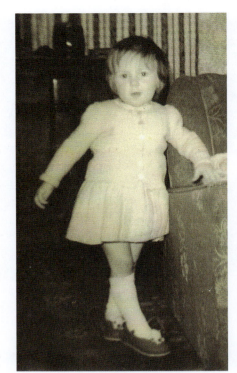

Author at Moorland Road

On holiday with mum 1959

Mum, Gran and I

Edith May Rawle (Gran), Aunty Glad, Grandad and I

Labour Party women's section circa 1950s

Feversham Avenue coach trip 1950s

Chapter two

Bramble, the dog from Wales.

The terraced house in Bridgwater was a noisy place to live in. It had a lane that backed onto the houses where lots of neighbourhood children ran up and down shouting. At one point a young boy threw part of a house brick over my fence and it hit Floyd squarely on the head, drawing blood. I spoke to his parents and asked them to stop him throwing bricks but after a day or two the dangerous play continued as usual. They then bought him a puppy and in the January snow the little creature was banished to their back garden to cry in the cold. Despite my pleas to them to let her into the house she was left in the garden freezing. Behind the lane lived a man my work collegue and I called D.I.Y. man. From the minute I moved in until I left, this man who didn't seem ever to leave his home was hammering and crashing about in his house and garden. With this and the feral children it became impossible to concentrate even long enough to read there. I decided to move out and asked Chris what he thought.

At the time mortgage rates fluctuated regularly and on my small income the mortgage and bills were becoming difficult to meet. Chris was on a low wage and reluctantly we decided that neither of us could afford to continue with a mortgage. I looked for a house to rent. Again neither of us could afford to rent seperately so we agreed to share and split the rent between us. This would avoid the need for me to rent a bedsit which would otherwise be all I could afford and where Floyd might not be welcome. We put the house up for sale. By then I had started to get painful back problems so it was Chris who had to redecorate the house. He dug the garden over too and I managed to plant it with lots of bright annual flowers so it might catch someones eye to sell. Chris painted the outside and with its fresh new decoration and front garden full of multi coloured opium poppies it didn't take long for someone to make us an offer.

On selling we managed to make a tiny profit each after repaying the mortgage and this went on removal costs and a deposit for the new house. The rental property was a semi detached nineteen thirties house in a long street near Bridgwater docks. It had a large back garden with an allotment next to it with greenhouse, shed and a field behind. By then I was an avid gardener. Due to increasing back problems I couldn't dig or weed but Chris was always happy to muck in. He rotavated the allotment and pulled up all the weeds. I chose the seeds, grew them in pots and kept an eye on them in the greenhouse until they were ready to plant out. Floyd loved her huge new garden and allotment. She spent hours chewing sticks on the lawn. Photos taken of her at the time show a glossy, mischievous young lady who looks a bit like Pan playing his pipes whilst biting her stick in the garden.

Just one street away there was a run of fields that led up to Wembdon village. This was a perfect place for Floyds walks. Three times a day I would walk with her along the narrow tarmac path that ran beside the fields. There were more deep rhynes but this time I didn't try to jump them. The fields didn't seem to be grazed much and the grass grew quite tall providing habitat for myriad insects. There were tall brown bulrushes at the edge of the rhynes where dragonflies hovered and damselflies flitted over the glittering water. Floyd and I listened to the buzz of bees and the chirp of crickets as we ambled along on these mellow afternoons. Whilst I kept to the path she would explore the edge of the fields searching for wildlife and reading the scents of animals who had passed there. When other dogs passed us Floyd greeted them amicably and with decorum. As well as being the perfect intuitive companion she was so well behaved I began to think I had become a very proficient dog carer and with this in mind set about looking for dog number two.

While we had been living in the rental property we became aware of a problem with the neighbour. Initially he seemed friendly enough. When we first moved in he actually climbed over our back garden fence to greet us. This made me feel very uneasy, as he did not seem to have much sense of other people's boundaries. As the months wore on he began making snide remarks about us and one evening he even banged on my wall shouting, "Dirty lesbians" when I had a girlfriend to stay.

Despite the proximity of the beautiful fields I felt unsettled in the town. With a love of the countryside and increasing irritation with the neighbour I began to fantasize about living out of town somewhere more rural. Maybe Wales where property might be cheaper. Once again Chris, who had nowhere to go if we gave up the rental house, agreed to come looking for a home. I had spoken to him about finding another dog to keep Floyd company and thought dog and house hunting could be combined. Armed with estate agents brochures we hired a car and drove to Wales. We had no wish to annoy the Welsh population by taking up housing needed by them, but I longed to find somewhere quiet to live, with maybe a bit of land at the back. We stuck a pin in the map and drove to Newquay leaving Floyd with a friend so we could explore at our leisure. I'd never been to Wales before and crossing the Severn bridge I was excited to see dual signs for the two languages as Chris drove along the roads. We would see 'Ar werth' every so often on a house for sale.

We saw a few nice houses we thought we could afford, one in particular might have suited. It was a tiny detached cottage all on its own. Miles from the nearest village. It was in desperate need of care and repair, but it had a garage, two gardens and its own little well. We could have our own water. I felt really excited looking around imagining what I could grow there. Realistically though it would cost more than we could borrow to do it up and there was no prospect of employment nearby. During the course of the day we came to the sad conclusion that our job prospects were not good and abandoned the house search to look for a dog instead.

While driving we passed an animal shelter. We drove back to the premises and said we were looking for a dog. When considering adoption I had decided to look for another Collie and as Floyd was still able to conceive I had decided against getting a male dog. Floyd hadn't been spayed because I considered it unnecessary surgery. She was never allowed out alone to get pregnant and while on heat we sprayed her with herbal preparations to mask hormonal smells that might interest other dogs. If we were to have another Collie in the house we would need to find a bitch. With this in mind we told the woman running the shelter what kind of dog we hoped to find. She looked at me thoughtfully. Looking back I wonder if she was wrestling with her desire to say something that might have put me off. "Well" she said slowly, pausing to look at the building behind her, "we've only got one dog on the premises that's a bitch. "You'd better come and look". The inside of the large building was filled with seperate runs. Each run seemed to have three dogs in it. From every direction big soft eyes twinkled at Chris and I. They seemed to be pleading for attention and a home. One lovely Collie stretched his paws through through the bars of the run to touch my sleeve as I walked past. I leaned down to speak to him. "How beautiful you are " I said. The kennel woman had stopped at the run opposite. " If it's a bitch you're after she's over here." I walked across to where she was standing at the end of a run from which a terrible gutteral noise was emanating. A snarling, white dog was pacing the pen and was about to bite the nose of a collie next to her. Another collie approached and the three of them were stood like cowboys ready to draw a gun around a bowl of food. One of the male dogs leaned in towards the dinner and his companion followed suite to take his share of the dog meat. A cacophony of noise broke out and frantic movement. Growls, snarls and snatches of teeth. Then suddenly all the food was gone. The male dogs retreated and the big white collie was licking her lips. I steadied myself on the bars of the pen saying " She doesn't take any prisoners." The big white Collie came to the edge of the run, I knelt down to talk to her. "You frightened me to death" I told her, looking at her carefully. While she'd been fighting she looked enormous. With the hackles on her neck stood up and her coat standing on end she looked twice her actual size. Once the incident was over I noticed she was actually a very beautiful dog. Her bright white coat was sprinkled with black mottling and she had enormous warm brown eyes. She stood next to me and began softly whittering and whistling. She seemed to be trying to explain something to me, this human stranger evaluating her from outside the bars. "She's a huge character and she isn't always fighting" said the kennel woman, presumably thinking this would be a selling point. Chris and I looked at each other and said nothing. We decided to take the bitch for a walk. "She's called Rambo" said the kennel woman, who I thought looked a little nervous.

Rambo burst out of her pen after her carer with a massive choke chain around her neck. This didn't inspire us with confidence. We walked along the lanes next to the kennels with her trying to guess if we would get along and how she would react with Floyd. Rambo was full of bluster. She walked with her coat puffed up to look fierce resembling a porqupine. She tugged on her lead quite forcefully and pulled Chris right into a hedge. I got a sinking feeling in my stomach thinking this wasn't the dog for me. Her coat was so busy to look at I wondered if it would give me a migraine. I was just going to say to Chris that I thought she might be too much of a handful for us, when a huge H.g.v. lorry sped past us. It slowed up by the corner of the road and as the driver decreased his speed, the air brakes on the lorry gave out a gigantic hiss. Huge puffed up Rambo jumped clean into the ditch and lay cowering and shaking, terrified of the noise. As I looked at her then I saw what I thought she was, a very young lady who had to fight to get her dinner. She had been rejected by her first family and was living in what amounted to a cage. A rush of pity engulfed me. "We'll have to take her home" I told Chris. "No one else will want her." The kennel woman refused to take any money for Rambo. At first she asked us for one pound, then as if fearing we might refuse even this token gesture she said, "Tell you what, have her for nothing, I'll even throw in the lead". She helped us load Rambo into the car briskly. Must get on" she said before we could change our minds. "Dogs to feed, dinner to get ready." She disappeared into her house. We gave Rambo a drink in the plastic bowl we had brought along in case and looked at the concrete sheds and dog pens. We were going to take Rambo home. She had left her cage forever.

The journey home would take a while and we weren't sure how Rambo felt about cars. We decided to stop at the beach at Newquay to let her stretch her legs before the long drive home. She seemed fine in the car. Very interested in looking out of the window. At the beach she sniffed along the sand and enjoyed herself in the pale sunshine. A welsh family approached. "That's a beautiful dog" said the father. We explained we had only just met her while his young son patted her coat. The little boy seemed entranced with her and Rambo seemed to be used to children. The child and dog ran around the beach until I thought it was time to drive home. "Come here Rambo" I said with misplaced confidence. "Come on we've got to go

21

home" Rambo's ears pricked up at the sound of her name, but she didn't move. The child said something to her in Welsh and when he stood next to us she came straight over. "She doesn't understand English" said the small boy, stroking her ears. "You'll have to speak to her in Welsh".

Challenge number one then in looking after Rambo was to learn to speak another language. I had an on off girlfriend who lived in Cardiff who had a smattering of Welsh. I asked her to come up with some phrases it would be useful to be able to say to a dog. We kept it simple and duly a letter arrived in the post. Conversations to have with a Welsh collie. Phrases in Welsh for me to learn included good girl, come here, stay, goodnight and dinner. This would have to do until I learnt Welsh, she understood English or we dispensed with speech and relied on body language.

The journey home had been uneventful. Rambo had kept her nose on the window and relished watching the countryside move past until we got back to Somerset. Once there I took her straight up to Wind down, a Forestry commission plantation with wide curving paths, good for dog walks. I let Rambo off the heavy, brutal choke chain and she sniffed around for some time until Chris arrived with Floyd. I knew Floyd would be fine with Rambo but I wanted them to meet in an outside space where neither thought they owned any territory. Floyd walked around ignoring Rambo entirely. Rambo rushed up to Floyd with her hackles up but Floyd appeared not to notice her and still sniffing around she walked off. This was a puzzle to Rambo who appeared to have expected some sort of stand off. After two hours of sniffing and walking with plenty of stops for a bowl of water each both dogs appeared to have accepted each other. On the way home in the car Floyd sat in the passenger foot well and Rambo sat in the back with a soft new lead and collar that Chris had brought.

At home we fed both dogs an evening meal. Floyd had long been used to eating her vegan food and Rambo wolfed it down fast with eyes darting around as if she thought someone might steal it. There was some food left in the pan and we gave her this as well. I had wondered if she would take to it but she just seemed grateful not to have to fight other dogs to get to her meal. When she had finished her food and Floyd was asleep on the sofa we let Rambo out into the garden, I don't think she had seen a lawn before and we left her rolling on the grass making contented noises.

Chris and I decided to change her name, I had no intention of walking in the fields shouting "Rambo, where are you?". We would call her something similar. We thought of names like Rambler and Bumble. Eventually we settled on Bramble. It sounded enough like Rambo that she would know we were talking to her without being such an unlikely name for a bitch. Going out into the garden to check on her and explain about the name change, I found her belching and licking her lips. Between her paws was an empty margarine tub. She had snuck into the kitchen quietly when Chris and I were talking, jumped up on the work surface and stolen an unopened carton of margarine from the cupboard. Now she was sitting on the lawn looking defiant, with margarine covering her nose. "Oh Bramble you'll make yourself sick" I told her. The brief ensuing silence where she stared into my eyes was broken by a loud expulsion of canine gas. This set the tone of our interactions.

Floyd was never a particularly territorial dog, she was happy to share the house with Bramble. Because Bramble was young she looked on Floyd partly as a mother figure. They had separate baskets and blankets, food, water and toys. Out walking I would throw a tennis ball to be fetched and Floyd would race after it, leap into the air and catch it on its downward arc. Bramble would stand still and open her mouth expecting the ball to drop in it. When it didn't she would run after Floyd copying her every move. She was learning from her all the time. On the whole things were working out well. They were at different developmental stages. Floyd was mature and intelligent, Bramble was impressionable and young.

Mostly they got on well. Once or twice there was a flare up of aggression. As Bramble grew bolder she challenged Floyd for space. Twice they fought and had to be seperated. Once as we held them apart Floyd struggled free and bit Brambles nose. This was after she had been attacked by her for reasons we didn't understand. Another time outside the house they began fighting when I was with them on my own. I tried to pull Bramble off of Floyd who she had launched herself at. As I got hold of her she spun her head round quickly and put a single tooth in the corner of my eye. It fitted under the lid painlessly and briefly. It didn't puncture my eye but was a clear warning to me that Bramble was serious about attacking Floyd and she was warning me to keep off. "Bramble." I shouted so loudly that she forgot she was supposed to be fighting. While she was momentarily distracted I grabbed her, picked her up, wrenching my back and put her into the back garden. Neither Floyd nor I were hurt but I would have to keep an eye on them together in the future. Although Chris and I were treating both dogs equally and ensuring they both had all they needed to live comfortably, I needed to adopt a new strategy to try to prevent further flare ups of canine tempers as Bramble grew into an adult dog.

Most of the time we walked the dogs together to facilitate bonding between them. I decided that maybe Bramble and I needed to bond more as individuals. To facilitate closeness between us we would have one walk extra each day together alone. Her other walks would be with Floyd as usual. Bramble and I would go to places she had not been before and hopefully this would improve our bonding. On her own without fear of competition for food or affection I found her to be a loving dog, eager to communicate who kept close to my side without her lead. I wondered if I had done either dog any favours bringing them together as they both enjoyed individual attention so much alone. Or perhaps Bramble needed more socialisation. With this thought in mind I decided to take her to an animal rights meeting in Bristol. It was to be held in a pub where some group members were squatting. Activists often brought companion animals along and I thought this might be a good place to assist in the socialisation of Bramble. With the permission of the householders I took her along to the meeting. She mostly lay quietly on the floor until the group began to disperse. Someone suggested we walk with our various dogs on some nearby green space. As we got up to go Bramble and another dog who had caught her eye, began to snarl and she leapt up to scare the other animal. The householder got very cross saying "I will not have dogs fighting in my house." Thus we left the meeting in shame and disgrace. It made me wonder if Bramble would be better on her own.

Time passed and we got into a routine. While walking with her Bramble got my full attention. She was not one for fetching things and appeared to believe if you were stupid enough to throw your own ball away you could fetch it yourself. With Floyd I had done a lot of training because that was what I had read an inexperienced dog owner should do. Later I got to thinking this was patronizing and controlling of the dogs. Whilst sit, stay and leave are important for safety I decided that where Floyd had been drilled in manners quite unnecessarily Bramble would be handled very differently. Floyd was always happy to sit at the kerb of a busy road when requested, Bramble couldn't see the point. Rather than set myself up for endless disagreements with Bramble I decided to treat her as I would another human. I was polite and non confrontational with her and always respected her space. She was never taught to do any pointless tricks to satisfy a human ego. I treated her like the equal I believe she was and explained things to her in terms I thought she could understand, I felt it was important to listen to what she had to say. Obviously this is mostly non verbal with dogs, it involves watching body language and understanding behaviours and actions.

Still we had confrontations. One of the places we enjoyed walking was on forestry commission land. At Wind down near Enmore there is a large swathe of forest with native trees and planted pine. The long winding path twists in a rough figure of eight. For our afternoon walks Bramble and I would often amble around the forest. Much of the time there was no one else about. Only the birds and an occasional deer for company. Bramble liked to look for squirrels who she wasn't fast enough to catch but that didn't stop her dancing round the base of tall trees barking at the vanishing creatures as they raced to the overhanging branches.

One afternoon when we were strolling quietly along I heard a hunt horn. This worried me because as well as knowing what happened to quarry I was always afraid the hunt hounds would attack Bramble and Floyd. Although we had only just got to Wind down I decided that we should turn back and go home in case Bramble was attacked by the hunt dogs. I turned to go and called her after me but she was having none of it and refused to walk back towards the car. While I was thinking of how to get her home without injury two long legged hounds appeared on the horizon. Neither took any notice of us but I still felt nervous, at any minute they could pounce on Bramble. I had to get her home. Just as I was about to try to pick her up she launched herself at the hounds with a furious bark, lips curled and snarling. Before it could escalate I managed to grab her, shouting at her to stop.

Bramble growled at me in fury, angry at having her will thwarted. She raged and snapped, desperate to get at the other dogs. The only way I could get her to budge was to tie my scarf round her like a harness and move her away inch by inch from the nonplussed hounds, holding her every step of the way. It took us forty minutes to walk the short distance back to the car with the wild creature snarling canine abuse at me. Once back in the car she reluctantly allowed herself to be persuaded to get in. Safely inside I locked the doors and let out a sigh of relief. We were both running with sweat after our battle of wills. I gave her some water and then told her off, "Bramble, what are we going to do with you?"

At home later the tension drained out of me as I talked to gentle and diffident Floyd who was carefully chewing a toy on the carpet. Chris had left a note saying he had walked with her. I lay down next to her and gave her a big hug. Bramble was snoring in her basket exhausted from her busy day. This was one of the many times over the years that I wondered if I'd done the right thing in homing her. At times when I felt like that I only had to remember that the day after I'd brought her back from Wales. There had been a flood that deluged the dog shelter, and along with all the other dogs the collie who had reached out to touch my sleeve, had drowned.

Chapter Three.

Bramble Speaks; Listening to dogs.

Bramble and I had been out in the fields at Hamp. Sunset gave us a rosy glow as we set back towards home covered in mud. My boots were decorated with wet leaves and Bramble was resplendent in some sort of awful slime she had found to roll in on her travels. I was wondering what the noxious pong on her could be when I realized she was no longer beside me. This was puzzling as she had been there only seconds before. As a mild wave of panic began to wash over me a woman came running out of her front door on the corner of our street shouting abuse at someone I couldn't see who seemed to be in the house behind her. "Is that your dog?" she raved as I drew level with her garden. Her expression of horror and flustered manner seemed to indicate she had received a visit from Bramble. "She just barged past me as I was opening the door and she's run in and sat down by the fire, I can't get her out" she said. Trailing mud and other debris from the boggy fields I tramped over her lovely carpet to persuade Bramble away from the cozy hearth she had settled down by. She grumbled at me in a deep voice as I guided her away. That was very typical of her behaviour when I first adopter her.

As a youngster she had been used to fighting for food and space. To her these things represented life and death. In the kennel where I found her there was one bowl of food for the dinner of three dogs. If she didn't fight she didn't eat. If she fought she risked injury and also experienced the fear of a vicious struggle for supremacy with two male dogs she had to share a run with after fighting. To Bramble every interaction to do with resources, be they food ,water or space, was a challenge to her survival and she was straight on the alert, ready to defend what she needed to keep her alive. There would have been no point in smacking her because that would have reinforced her fear about aggression around resources. What I did was feed her seperately from Floyd. They each had water, food and beds in different parts of the house. Most of the time they could happily share the living space together but at meal times or where I perceived there might be points of tension, like the vet's surgery, I kept Bramble and Floyd apart.

People often say "If only animals could talk". I believe they do communicate their feelings to us but canine communication is very different from ours. Their perception of the world differs from that of humans. We are largely visual creatures, our eyesight, unless we are blind, will be for most of us our primary source of information gathering for our brains to process. With dogs their prominent sense is smell. A rough guide to the difference between human and canine sense of smell would be that a dogs sense is said to be one million times more sensitive than that of a person. A dogs perception of the world then would be based more on what she smells than what she sees. Exceptions might be so called sight hounds like Salukis. Individual animals will vary due to breed and health status, but on the whole the way a dog experiences the world will be lead by her olfactory senses.

In my experience dogs will understand intentions by watching what you are doing via body language rather than just by listening to you. I believe they do understand language but can be bored and confused by long sentences. They will listen for key words like walk or biscuit rather than take in everything you say. Dogs respond to verbs. The part of the sentence that tells them what is happening. Keeping spoken communication brief and to the point is key to allowing a dog to get the meaning of speech and keeping her interest. Another thing that differs between dogs and humans is our perception of time. On average most dogs will live to around fourteen years old, although this varies with breed. The large breeds tend to live shorter lives. That means that dogs move from being a puppy, to youngster, mature dog and elderly creature in what to humans is a relatively short space of time. All of the dogs in my care have learnt to say something that sounds like "Hurry". None of them could pronounce the letter aitch, so it always sounded like "urry" but to me this indicates that dogs find humans very slow in our movements and thought processes. I believe this can lead to boredom for dogs. Every human year lived is said to represent approximately seven years to a dog, that means that every hour lived seems like seven hours to a dog. This difference in the perception of time and of life lived means that dogs may become frustrated by what they perceive as the slow speed at which humans live our lives. If left alone at home a dog will experience that period of time as being much longer than a human does.

In terms of caring for dogs this means if you are trying to give a dog a life that fits in with her physiology or psychology it is helpful to fit routines around a time frame that will fit in with a dogs sense of time. When I had Bramble and Floyd living with me I tried not to leave them alone for long either together or seperately. Chris mostly did night shifts so if I was going out for a while he was on hand to care for the dogs. Floyd and Bramble had, what I called four maintenance walks a day, early morning, midday, late afternoon and late evening. Each walk was thirty five minutes, this gave them time to relieve themselves, stretch their legs and enjoy being outside of the house. Then either Chris or I would take them out to the fields for a much longer foray each day. The rest of the time the back door would be open to the garden for them to amble in and out as they pleased. If a dog is left in a house alone it will probably feel like, and indeed be, a prisoner. Dogs are outdoor creatures that we have decided to keep indoors. We owe it to them to keep letting them out. Ill health and neurotic behaviour are one result of not enough exercise or freedom. They need to be able to ramble around smelling the scent messages left by other dogs. These are likely to be communications of canine perceptions of status, the ownership of geographical areas and health

Luckily most people will never see the inside of a police cell. Those that have been incarcerated in one for even a small amount of time will tell you that being locked into a space somewhere you cannot exit of your own free will feels very oppressive indeed. Imagine then a lifetime of being a prisoner of others from a few weeks after birth until you die. Or maybe having several homes. Shunted from one to another, with no say over how you are treated or where you are made to stay or go. To effectively have all meaningful choice taken from you. Complicate this by being abducted from your mother by alien species, much of whose behaviour and communication you do not understand. If you are lucky you are fed, watered and allowed to excercise without being beaten. If you are unlucky you may be physically hurt, terrorised, teased, abused or neglected. Still you are stuck in your prison with no way out. After a while all hope will go, you may become depressed or submissive to the whims of the prison warder that keeps you. This is, in my opinion the psychological landscape that captive animals have to endure. Even with the best will in the world and the kindest owners these animals are in our homes at our behest and in this they have no choice. While I do not believe you can ever own an animal I use this word to describe someone who keeps one because the phrase companion animal used by animal rights activists doesn't tell the story of the animals lack of choice in the situation. The dog in your home can never say "I've had enough of you" and just walk away.

One of the things I noticed when I first adopted Floyd was her fear of walking on the lawn at the back of the house. When I tried to explain to her it was okay to use it to urinate on she wouldn't go near it. When I picked her up and put her on it she leapt off in terror. At some point she may have been hit or scolded for walking on a lawn. With each new carer a dog has there are new rules and compromises for the animal to learn. What may have been permissable in one house may be frowned on in another. Bramble would always lunge for our hands if we went near her dinner, even to put a bit more on the plate. Instead of telling her off and teaching her to stop lunging at us by repeatedly taking the food away from her, as recommended by some dog trainers, we just didn't go near her food while she was eating. Taking her plate or a dog bowl away would just reinforce her fear and teach her to be submissive. I did not want submissive dogs.

If the dog you care for exhibits aggression around food I feel it is better to leave her alone when she's eating. Imagine how you might feel if someone bigger than you took your dinner away until you learned to be polite. Aggression in dogs is mostly fear based, be it protective of dinner or where an animal is trying to establish dominance with another dog. She is trying to ensure the means of her survival and the way to deal with this is to defuse the situation depending on the circumstances. It never helps to hit an animal.

One way in which I believe dog care can be vastly improved, promoting canine longevity, is by looking at human attitudes to other animals and specifically dogs. Floyd and Bramble were always treated at least as my equals. My lingering suspicion was that they might be vastly superior on many counts to me. Whatever the case I treated them respectfully, as I would treat another human. They were spoken to kindly but without patronisation. They were never made to learn or perform tricks which only feeds the human ego. Within the structure of our lives and what we humans needed to do to survive such as to fetch food, work, pay bills etc, we tried to facilitate the dogs to have as much autonomy as possible. If they wanted to go for a particular walk we would follow in their direction. If they didn't want to be groomed in the morning it could wait until the afternoon. If Floyd had seen enough of Bramble, or vice versa for the day, they were free to retire to their individual rooms. Both dogs had their own bedrooms. At some point in their lives they both had comfy baskets until one time Bramble decided she preferred the bed belonging to Chris. When this happened he had to put up with Bramble commandeering his space and pushing him towards the floor. Later the dogs had their own single divan beds with pillows and blankets. They enjoyed being able to stretch out full length as we do. Because Chris and I always tried to treat the dogs we cared for as equal to ourselves we would never put a dog in a position that would be viewed as an inappropriate situation for a human. They were never subjected to people, old or young, that they found stressful. No lively children or abusive adults. If we were in a situation where there were likely to be obnoxious people the dogs were kept away. They were not left in the car for hours in car parks or outside of shops because this would have stressed them or endangered their health. Even when the weather is not too hot dogs will experience boredom and fear left alone in a car, again they are prisoners if locked in a vehicle. Feelings of powerlessness and anxiety may result which leads to stress and ill health. Allowing animals the freedom to move around, be outside and not feel trapped and powerless are essential if you want a dog to live a long life.

It can be hard for humans to understand that the mental health of an animal affects longevity. People often think that if an animal is fed and watered that is all they need to do for her. An example would be caged rabbits, people buy them for children, stick them in hutches and most of the time that is where they are forced to stay. If lucky they may get put in a run on a lawn. Rabbits are social creatures. In the wild they live in burrows with extended family and run free all day. Sticking them in a rabbit hutch, alone or with one companion is unnatural. People leave them in hutches for their entire lives sometimes. Imagine how that must feel. No company. No room to move. No grass to nibble. Just years of utter tedium and hopelessness. I would like to see this practice banned. It is much the same for dogs if you put them in a house and they don't get out enough to excersise. They need fresh air, companionship and purpose. Most breeds need to be active and engaged. They can be involved in your life as with Floyd who enjoyed helping in the garden. They also need their own pastimes like the space and time to explore new places, or being able to spend time with other dogs.

I believe dogs are better being educated rather than trained. Training has slave connotations. Training a dog to do your bidding is an interaction where the trainer has control and is imposing their agenda on an animal. What gives them the right to do that? I agree with cultivating sensible habits for safety reasons, like teaching a young dog to be careful at a roadside or learning to stay because there are situations where safety requires that. Otherwise I do not believe in training dogs. Educating them and allowing them to educate you is better. Learning to communicate with dogs is an important first step. Converse with them, not at them. This involves learning about dog behaviour. How they communicate and why. Floyd, for example would point things out to me by walking to them and walking back to me highlighting an object she wanted. Once at a garden centre she did this with a childs tennis set. When I didn't fetch it for her she fetched it herself and I had to go and pay for it. My Alsatian friend, Dreadlock would point his nose at things he wanted, a friends dog would just go and stand next to things until his human worked out what he was saying. This is basic stuff but a lot of people miss it. Because dogs don't verbalise in the way people do we often do not understand what they are trying to tell us, or we miss their communications altogether. These signals are often subtle and small. If you want to understand dogs you need to spend time watching their behaviour and learning to interpret these signals. Often this will be as simple as the dog looking at something she wants then looking back at you, or it may be auditory with barking, whistling or otherwise vocalising something the dog wants. People make the mistake of thinking they are smarter than dogs because they fail to understand what the dog is trying to tell them. I am sure dogs have their own ideas about who is smarter in this situation.

Smell also plays a large part in dog communication and because human sense of smell is vastly inferior to that of dogs we are destined to miss out on what is probably the most important form of communication with dogs. Although we can use it at times to communicate where we might be taking the dog, for example by keeping a favourite stick she found on the beach and letting her smell it when that is where you are going to go. In this way the smell of objects stand in for words. Sign language can be used with dogs also they will watch your movements and can learn to derive meaning from that. You can also guage intention by watching your dogs body language and habits. Remember that behaviour will vary with dogs, even of the same breed due to different circumstances, socialisation and genetic makeup. If you have more than one dog in the house you will need to work harder to connect with your dogs emotional landscape. For example at one point I had three Collies living together at my house. When Bramble was older we adopted two other collies, a bitch called Sally and a dog called Stan. At this time Bramble was slower than when we adopted her to be with Floyd who she outlived. Sally was from a village where I had been house hunting. I didn't buy a house but I did find a family looking to rehome their dog. Due to the owners occupation with their children Sally had not had much exercise, although in other ways she had been well looked after. The man who gave her to us had bought her before he was married and she had very good self esteem. She came into our house considering herself very much the top dog. Bramble was an older citizen by then and the male dog Stan, was very quiet and timid. Sally decided she was the boss dog. This was not a situation Bramble had encountered before. All of her life she had been the Alpha female. In old age she accepted that Sally was stronger and fitter and we had to be careful that this did not lead to any bullying of Bramble by Sally.

Stan had been a vagrant dog, thrown onto the streets by a previous family. He was trusting of us but very shy and decided to be very quiet and passive around the two assertive female dogs.
There was then lots of power play to negotiate around whilst working out what communication was going on between the dogs, and what was withheld for political expediency. In this situation Sally would articulate in whatever form that took, what she wanted. Bramble would be more hesitant and need some encouragement, and Stan would have to be watched to see what he needed because it was not always apparent when he was with Bramble and sally. "What do you want Bramble?" would often work. She

would walk in a circle if she wanted to go to the park or lick her lips if it was food she wanted. Stan would need to be seperated from the bitches and he would then go to what he wanted, like the door or the biscuit box, and stand next to it. Some people instinctively recognise these communications in animals, some can learn to understand and others will be too insensitive and their dogs lives will be poorer for it.

After Floyd had died I acquired a German Shepherd who Chris named Dreadlock. Dreadlock was frankly smarter than Chris or I and he decided to train us. He probably didn't realise it was going to take him so long. By the time Dreadlock arrived I had moved to another terraced house in a challenging street in the town. It was on a long road with a traffic roundabout at one end and the railway station at the other. People used it as a through road to other places. On Friday and Saturday nights many drunks would pass through it shouting abuse and fighting, vehicles would be damaged and the occasional window broken. Dreadlock hated our street. When we first moved in to the house he walked from room to room upstairs and down evaluating the layout. In my bedroom he pushed the curtains aside with his nose to look down on the back garden to check where any breaches of security might occur. When he was satisfied he knew the location of all the exits and doors he needed to guard, he settled down in the kitchen at the back which he chose as his domain. Bramble, Sally and Stan chose the front room for their baskets by lying in there and falling asleep.

We always had to keep a door shut between the collies and Dreadlock because the two females would boss the enormous Alsatian around if we didn't. Dreadlock decided that although the house could be guarded safely he didn't trust the street. With its noisy drunks and troublesome youths, broken glass and damaged vehicles he decided to avoid walking through it. For a while when I moved there he would allow Chris to walk him from the house to the park two streets away, but later he refused to walk down the street at all. He was a big heavy dog, seven stone in weight and as tall as Chris when he stood on his hind legs and put his paws on his shoulders. He would let Chris take him outside the door but he would refuse to walk anywhere. Dreadlock would lie down on the pavement and would refuse to budge until Chris or I allowed him to jump into my car and drive him somewhere nice to walk. A trip along the canal or river bank would be fine but he especially enjoyed the forest trail at Enmore. For a while we took him in the car but Dreadlock was not a big fan of men for reasons best known to himself. If Chris moved while in the car Dreadlock would give him a stern look and give a very deep growl in his throat. This was enough to keep Chris in his place frozen to the seat. Clearly this was unpleasant for Chris so we bought a bigger vehicle to take Dreadlock out in and this had enough space for everyone. Dreadlock had succeeded in training us not to walk him through what he clearly viewed as the perilous streets and had even slowly persuaded me to buy a bigger vehicle. All this probably took him longer than he had anticipated to teach us because with humans things obviously take a while to sink in. He got his result though and enjoyed his many trips out in his van with his head stuck out the window and the breeze rippling through his long fair fur.

Brambles communication was all about body language if she wanted to tell us something. On Sundays she was always taken to the beach. when she thought it was time to leave the house she would walk in a circle and stand by the door doing a little jig where she jumped about much as lambs do in the spring. This was her signal that meant beach walk. Some communication then is subtle and can be small eye movements looking towards a desired object, or something much more obvious like Dreadlocks point blank refusal to walk down a road he considered unsafe. It takes time to get to know individual dogs and their vocabulary of signs and signals. What you can understand from them will be a mix of what you are able to notice and interpret and what they want you to know. Like humans dogs may not always be entirely open about their behaviour.

When Floyd and Bramble were younger another dog came to stay with us. She was an English sheepdog cross who had been poorly treated. She had never been taken for a walk and had been fed on cheap fatty food which made her obese and lumbering. Her fur had fallen out due to malnutrition and neglect. She belonged to a family I knew. The son had bought her for the father who had no intention of walking her and could not afford to feed her properly. They called her "Myth". On visiting them one afternoon I was so incensed to see the state of her I took her home and refused to give her back. The father of the family didn't object. It was a worry off his hands. Once Myth was at my place I started to feed her the rice and T.V.P. diet. For the first time in her life she got lots of walks as Chris gallantly took her out. She became fit and lean and her fur grew back. The only trouble was Bramble didn't like her. Floyd had known Myth since Myth was a puppy and they occasionally played in Myths back garden so Floyd had no problem with her. Myth had not met Bramble but was friendly to her when I took her home. Bramble seemed okay with Myth and on the surface of it everything was okay. After Myth had lived with us for a while a disturbing pattern began to emerge. Despite at least five walks each day with Chris, to relieve herself, big lumps of faeces began to appear overnight and we found them on the conservatory floor in the morning. Neither Bramble or Floyd had ever done this in the house so I assumed it must be Myth. Every morning for a week I found more poo and would grumble about it as I put it on the compost heap in the garden. I could not help noticing Bramble looked very pleased with herself when I moaned about what I thought was Myths mess to Chris. An uncharitable thought occured to me. Perhaps the lumps were not Myths doing at all. Perhaps they were done by someone who was hoping Myth would become unpopular in the house. That night I kept an eye out looking in the conservatory quietly every now and then and I saw the culprit next to a steaming pile of mess on the floor. The culprit was Bramble. I told her I was unimpressed and she appeared to be a little crestfallen that I had discovered her ruse. It did point out to me though that Bramble was unhappy with Myth sharing her space. I had never intended to take Myth on forever because I could not afford three lots of veterinary fees or food long term, but she couldn't have stayed where she was getting fatter and more bald by the day. Myth went to a new home with someone who was looking for an old English sheepdog cross and in my house once again the conservatory floor went back to being clean in the morning. Bramble hadn't felt threatened enough by Myth to attack her, but she made her feelings very clear about how she was forced to share her space. This was an obvious communication of her feelings once I was able to understand what she was saying. Thus it is with dogs. They will speak to you and you can hear them. It just will not be in a language you are used to and if you want the information they are trying to give, you will have to learn to read the signs.

Bramble and Floyd at Shepton Mallet

Chapter Four.

Vets; Negotiating a health plan.

Dreadlock loved his old gas van. Too big to sit in the front, he had a comfy bed in the back of his long wheel base Ford Transit. Most times Chris or I would drive him up to the forest for his walks. In the afternoons one or other of us would pull up at Wind down and open the side door of the van for him to jump down to the mud track that lead around the plantation.

Wind down has the advantage of being peaceful and rural, with long straight paths where dog walkers can see each other coming from some distance ahead. This can be useful for a dog who prefers his own company. Dreadlock was such a dog. For this reason there were places where we knew we would meet other dogs where we would keep him on a lead. In other deserted spots he could be let off to explore without having the bother of dragging his person around behind him.

One afternoon Chris returned from walking with Dreadlock looking troubled. "Dreadly doesn't seem right" he said. He couldn't explain specifically what was wrong but felt Dreadlock was tired and walking more slowly than usual.

We booked a vets appointment and took him in that evening. Dreadlocks vet in Taunton was called Alistair. A thoughtful guy with a calm presence. He examined Dreadlock thoroughly then said he would run some tests. Dreadlock needed to have a scan. He was given an injection to make him sleepy. This worried me because the vet said it would slow his heart. The big dog lay on the floor with his head between his paws and became very quiet. His large, black ringed, brown eyes lost focus. The vet and his helper, assisted by Chris lifted Dreadlock up onto the table and started to scan his recumbent body. Alistair pointed to an area on the scanner that looked different from the rest. He said "Dreadlock has an unusual growth on his spleen, it may be cancer or it could be a cyst. The only way to be sure is to open him up". He warned us that because of Dreadlocks age he might not recover from the anesthetic. Unfortunately if left the lump might grow and if it was a cyst it could burst. Dreadlock would probably die.

I hadn't seen any of this coming. One minute my gentle, old friend was walking and well then we were told he might need surgery. Ever the ditherer regarding medical help I didn't know what to do for the best. We told Alistair we would think about the options and get back to him.

Chris and I talked round the subject for days. Neither of us were keen to lose Dreadlock under anaesthetic. At thirteen years old he was coming to the end of his life. An average age for an Alsatian to live is twelve. Dreadlock had already surpassed that. At the same time we didn't want him to die suddenly and in pain from a possible burst cyst.

We dithered some more then took him back to the vets surgery to talk again. Alistair wasn't around. The locum vet who stood in for him recommended we open Dreadlock up there and then so he could look at the lump direct. He said he would leave us alone in the waiting room for ten minutes so we could make a decision. Chris was all for leaving well alone. "The vets just bored" he raved. "I'm not letting some perishing vet open him up just because he's got nothing to do in the afternoon." He began to disparage the vets professionalism and character quite loudly' until I pointed out he was

38

stood in front of the c.c.t.v. camera. Probably the vet had heard everything he'd said. We remained undecided which is my motto in a sense. When in doubt do nothing. We told the vet we would think some more, keep an eye on the size of the lump vie Alistair, but for now we wouldn't put Dreadlock through the trauma of an operation.

This was a hard time for Chris and I. Dreadlock was getting old and this might be the health problem that caused his death. On the bright side he was still here so we needed to make the latter part of his life as pleasant as possible and enjoy him while we could.

I asked Chris to change his work hours so he could be off every afternoon. At the time Chris was working in residential care with flexible hours. His workplace juggled his hours so he could take the afternoons off. Everyday we would carefully load the old Alsatian into his van and drive slowly up to Wind down.

For a few days after diagnosis and possibly due to a virus Dreadlock picked his way gingerly around the forest circuit. He had slowed up, which gave me an idea. "Lets make a den for him" I proffered to the suggestible Chris.

At Enmore there are lots of off shoots from the forest path. We found one quite near where we parked the van that led down and around to a small, quiet glade. It was fringed with giant fir trees that towered above the native species and we sat down on a log looking for a spot to build a den. Next to the tallest fir was a sturdy bush with a tall central core. It looked like it would be a good spot for a den in the shape of a wigwam. Dreadlock and I looked around for logs and sticks for Chris, who had less back trouble than me, to haul back to the bush. He placed them around it at an angle resting in the branches of the bush. For a roof we collected fallen pine branches still covered in spiky, pungent needles. The den took a few days to slowly build. At last it was ready. We put in a waterproof sheet and some blankets and it was ready for dreadlock to try. In case he didn't understand what it was for Chris began to crawl in on his hands and knees to show him where to lie. Dreadlock, who always liked a game, strolled into the den knocking Chris flat on the floor and sat on him. Chris said "I think he knows what it's for".

Dreadlock loved his den. For two hours every afternoon he would access the little track that winds down to the glade in his bolt hole amongst the wildlife. He worked out that by sticking his long velvety nose through the branches of the den he could watch the fauna unseen. Next to the den, high in the big fir tree there was a squirrel. Dreadlock spent fascinated hours watching her run up and down the tree. I believe he thought if he waited long enough the squirrel would run into his den near enough to ambush. Time in the den gave us the space to contemplate what was going on. Dreadlock might not be with us much longer. These were precious hours to help him enjoy the sunset of his life before it came to an end. Much of the time I felt desperately sad that the time to say goodbye to a dog was drawing near again. It never gets any easier.

In the meantime we had the forest and some precious time to share. At Wind down during the winter it became very frosty. Chris and I would wrap ourselves in umpteen layers of clothes to try to keep the cold out. Commonly I would wear eight tops, four pairs of trousers and two overcoats. We must have looked like barrel people as we ambled along the paths. One time whilst resting in the freezing forest we noticed a bird of prey hovering over our heads attracted by the thermal heat of our hand warmers. It was often so cold we would wear two balaclavas, one full face and one as a liner to stop the wind making the skin on our faces hard and raw.

For all the extremes of weather the forest was an inspiration. Often we found ourselves alone in this winter wonderland. The earth would be solid and icy under our feet with sparkling white frost glittering on the branches of the trees. When there was snow on the forest floor it would often appear to be pink reflecting the setting sun.

To amuse ourselves Chris and I would make up stories about faerie folk who live in the forest. Elves and trolls and sinister hobgoblins. We became adept at spotting the real inhabitants of the woods. In the early evening we could watch the deer move across the forest floor grazing before sunset. One day I spotted a small, slow moving creature whose head was almost as big as her body. She was a tiny dormouse who had just woken up.

The forest was always full of birds. We came to recognise the calls. A Robin adopted us, we named him Sweetie. Sweetie was known by the locals for accompanying people around the forest circuit while they were walking their dogs. The fearless little robin began to groom us by following us around with his charming company. I began to bring bird food for him, hanging seeds and fatty balls on some of the native trees.

We got into a routine of doing a small circuit of the forest and sitting down for a rest. We would bring snacks and eat them on a log, with Dreadlock at our feet eating his daily banana. He liked to pick it up and shake the yellow fruit to make sure it was dead. I always found that endearing, he didn't want his banana to suffer as he ate it. Then he would settle down to chew one of his toys while Chris and I took out the wild bird food for Sweetie. Most of the time the little robin would eat it and then fly around us, bowing on tree branches as if to thank us for his food. Sometimes a fat, grey squirrel would get to the fatty balls first then Sweetie would have nothing to peck while we watched him. He became very tame and sometimes he brought friends along. Once he appeared with a tiny wren who we fed, and another time he brought Mrs. Robin and another small male along.

Time was ticking on. At first when Dreadlocks lump appeared we thought we would lose him immediately but the wheel of the year turned and soon it was Autumn once again. Wrapped up in our thermal layers with our den, Dreadlock and the wildlife we began to relax a bit. Perhaps we wouldn't lose our friend yet. For two more years we trod through drifts of autumn leaves and Dreadlock walked with us under the chestnut trees. We rolled nut shells to him covered in spikes and he growled at them when they prickled his nose. We had a few longer walks, taken gently in winter sunshine until one day something started to go wrong. We had slowly completed half a circuit of the woods when I realised Chris and Dreadlock had dropped back behind me. Sweetie had been flying with us and he kept wittering at me and disappearing away again back to where Chris and Dreadlock had stopped.

After waiting for some minutes I retraced my steps on the muddy path, Chris was standing over Dreadlock who as lying on the floor. "He just stopped" said Chris "I can't get him to move". The light was beginning to fade and although the forest is small it would be dangerous to negotiate the slippery path if we couldn't see our way. We waited several minutes to see if Dreadlock would be able to resume his walk but he stayed lying quietly and we couldn't coax him up. Chris tried to encourage him to stand by supporting his legs but Dreadlock slid back towards the floor. " I can't carry him" Chris said, stating the obvious, "I don't understand what's wrong". Dreadlock had started off okay but gradually tired. Perhaps he had just overtaxed his strength. It was a fair way back to the car with a large, tired dog to contend with. After trying to think of several unlikely solutions, such as quickly building a platform from branches to try to pull him along, we settled for the only thing we could think of that would work. We took off our various coats and jumpers and made an object, part sledge part sling. We put it gently underneath Dreadlock and Chris pulled him carefully up the incline towards the car. The light was fading fast and our clothes were caked in mud. Dreadlock came off of the coats once or twice and Chris coaxed him back on. After twenty slow minutes of effort we got back to the car and Chris managed to get our heavy friend in it.

We drove home in silence both thinking it was the end of the line for Dreadlock. At home Chris brushed the dried mud from his coat and we watched him as he ate his dinner. Looking at him walk to sit on his bed we noticed his back legs looked weak, they were slightly bent under him as if he couldn't hold his weight. We took him back to the vet. Alistair said that possibly his back had started to fuse. Eventually he would be unable to walk. On the up side the lump on his spleen felt smaller, it had actually started to shrink. From tennis ball size it had reduced to golf ball. Neither Chris nor I knew whether to laugh or cry, Dreadlocks legs were going but his lump was shrinking. We were so relieved that we had managed to allow him to avoid an operation. "Just think" said Chris unkindly referring to the locum vet "If we had let Boris the butcher at him he'd be dead now".

Gradually Dreadlocks mobility began to worsen. The vet said he didn't think our friend was in pain. Walking was becoming a problem though. Dreadlock would start off okay at the beginning of his walk but slow up after a while and be unable to walk home. This is the point, we thought, that most people would euthanise a dog. Neither Chris nor I ever considered it. No one would think of killing a human because she couldn't walk, neither would we consider putting Dreadlock down. He still ate his food with gusto and loved his comfy times at home. As we weren't going to let the vet kill him we had to think of a plan to facilitate his mobility.

We decided to try hydrotherapy but this was not destined to be. Dreadlock had one session but despite loving water he didn't like people.

The therapist at the pool tried to assist us in helping him access the water, but Dreadlock with his distaste for humans other than his pack couldn't stand being touched. He made it very clear that he wasn't going to be helped by a stranger and ended up getting stressed. The vet said, on balance, given his attitude to people it would cause more anxiety than it was worth. This was disappointing. We needed another plan. While we were parked on the town bridge in the van one Saturday Chris found a childs pushchair for sale. A bargain, five pounds in the charity shop. He mysteriously bought it and we took it home where he began to break it up. He wrenched the top off, keeping the wheels and structure. On top of this he fixed a flat, heavy board which he covered with a padded yoga mat. "Viola" he said "a carriage for Dreadly". At this point Dreadlock could still walk but his legs were getting weaker. Chris trained him to climb on to the pushchair carriage with a little help from friends. From the first minute he sat on it Dreadlock was delighted. He had no qualms about moving without effort and showed no fear.

Chris and I began to take the carriage to Wind down. Dreadlock and his transport were loaded into the van carefully. The carriage would be tied to the back so it didn't run into its cargo. Where Dreadlock has been traversing hesitantly round the edge of the woods he could now sail past on his new four wheeled transport. Chris had put a handle on it and pulled our friend along. Part of the forest path is a gentle slope and Dreadlock would sail down it with his eyes wide open, the wind in his fur and a mischevous grin. If Chris slowed up the pace, because pulling Dreadlock uphill was heavy work, he would bang his paw on the trolley. His way of increasing the speed.

The carriage was a success. Due to his size and failing strength a wheeled harness that strapped to him wouldn't have worked but on his trolley carriage he gained a new lease of life. Now his body could keep up with his brain. Dreadlocks life took on the breath of adventure again.

Our wild and wonderful friend lived for one more year after Chris made him his trolley. On his last sortie into the hills it was a beautiful summer day. Chris was pulling Dreadlock along the incline away from the tall fir trees, the sun was beating down and flies flew around Dreadlocks face. Chris parked the trolley in the shade of an overhanging branch along the last lap of our circuit. I had a video camera with me borrowed from Bridgwaters tiny film studio, the Engine room. I knew my old friend and companion of many years was coming up to his end. Speaking to him softly I filmed him for a few seconds lying in the shade. We then decided, so as not to over tax his strength that we should take him home. I filmed Dreadlock being pulled for what I didn't know at the time was his last day out. As he was pulled past the trees he looked up at a Beech that had a honeysuckle climbing up into its canopy. The highly scented flowers exuded their fragrance onto the breeze. Dreadlock grinned wolfishly as the trolley started up again, a little faster as it trundled to the base of the hill. As I filmed my old friend surveying the breadth of his territory I recognised some signal his body language had given. He did not expect to come back this way again.

Once at home Dreadlock fell asleep after a hearty meal and a hug from me. I knew our time together was running out. Gradually his strength was waning like a candle standing in a breeze. I slept on the kitchen floor that night next to my beautiful friend. When I woke I was aware of dreading what the day would bring. I said good morning to Dreadlock adding that in five minutes I would get up to give him a hug. Presently Chris trundled in from his bedroom and helped me sit Dreadlock up leaning against my legs and he fetched him a drink of water. As Dreadlocks head moved near the bowl of liquid he suddenly became limp. He was still breathing but he was falling asleep. Chris called the vet as an emergency and a man we didn't know came from the surgery bringing a young woman we had not met before. I felt like they had come mob handed because Dreadlock always barked at the vets. If they had come expecting him to give them any trouble they were mistaken. Dreadlock died in my arms just before the vet rang the doorbell. On his face was the most gentle of smiles and his eyes held no fear. He died with his human which is what I think he wanted. After Chris saw the vet out I lay on the floor next to Dreadlock. I put my arms around my enormous friend and buried my face in his soft yellow hair. Then I told him how much I loved him. I said to Chris "Do you think his death caused him any pain?" Chris replied " The vet said he doesn't think so and Dreadly was smiling. At death endorphin's flood the brain". So it seems Dreadlocks death was peaceful and he left the earth safe in my arms.

The reason I have told you this story is to illustrate that there are always various ways to handle a crisis in health. We could have put Dreadlock down at the vets when the lump on his spleen was discovered. He could have been operated on and died under anaesthetic. His lump or cyst could have burst but it didn't. Even if he survived an operation at that age it would have been traumatic, and we had of course had a cancerous lump taken from Floyd well into her old age. My feeling is that every situation is different. Every animal has her or his own health profile and quota of strength. Where Floyd was still lively despite her age Dreadlock was slowing up. We felt Floyd could handle an operation and it gave her another year of life, seven years to a dog. Dreadlocks strength was diminishing and we decided not to put him through surgery because we thought he was better without. So it proved as his lump diminished.

I have great respect for vets who train longer than doctors, but they don't know everything. My approach to vets has always been to err on the side of caution with a sick dog. I have always taken animals to the vet to get a diagnosis but don't always agree on the treatment. I always ask lots of questions and then research what I am told. Sometimes vets make mistakes.

As a young dog Dreadlock had an uncertain temper. Whilst he was gentle with me he would sometimes lunge at Chris. He seemed to be in pain. Taken to his first vet he was repeatedly prescribed antibiotics. They didn't help his suffering .I phoned German Shepherd rescue and spoke to a man who knew about Alsatians. He told me that a lot of that breed have a condition called pancreatic insufficiency. They need probiotics and enzymes to help their gut. Once I was aware of this we gave Dreadlock what he needed sprinkled on his rice. It made a huge difference to his health and comfort and the bellyache caused by his condition stopped. His temprement changed overnight and our grumpy, snappy friend turned into a big softie; at least with us. It always pays to read up on things yourself. There is often more than one way to solve a problem. If we had just kept giving Dreadlock the antibiotics he would have lived his life in constant pain as well as becoming immune to them eventually.

Medicine for animals changes over decades. In the 1980's pest control for fleas included the use of organo phosphates. These were later found to cause problems to animals and humans. Personally I worry about today's current flea controls. They are strong chemicals that may affect the health of cats and dogs.

Herbal remedies have their place. None of the vegan dogs in my carer ever showed any signs of worms nor were they regularly given worm powder. Chemicals in some of these preparations may affect dogs kidneys over time.

I favour a mixed approach to dog health. First you have to get diet right. I believe it is as important to be as careful what you don't give a dog to eat as what you do. As you can build health by appropriate feeding, so you can destroy it by feeding your dog things that are injurious to health. Commercial dog meats are mostly slaughterhouse by products. I believe dogs thrive better on vegan food. The vegan diet I fed Bramble on enabled her to live to twenty five years old, and Floyd to twenty. Dreadlock made fifteen which is good for a shepherd. If you build health you go to the vets less. When you get there ask lots of questions and do your research. You may decide the health problem a dog presents is straight forward and you are happy with your veterinary care. On the other hand many issues are complex with no easy answer. Sometimes you may feel a diagnosis is wrong. You know your canine friends and may have a gut feeling that something is not as it should be.

One of the dogs I cared for started biting the base of her tail. She was given lots of flea control and other paraphernalia, the biting continued and when she bit she cried. I kept taking her back to the vet worried that she had cancer. A while later it was diagnosed. She had no symptoms early on and she hadn't lost any weight but I'd seen Floyd years before succumb to the disease and in my guts I felt that was what was wrong. The point is if in doubt research, have a scan done, go back if you think a diagnosis is wrong. Conversely if repeats of medication are no help with a condition, try something else. I'm not advocating dumping your vet or diagnosing with no training, but you can observe, read and think your way around veterinary problems, while feeding to build health in dogs in your care. There are no hard and fast rules. Sometimes you must listen to vets, but sometimes it's best to listen to your instincts.

Chapter Five.

Floyd Dies.

Floyd lived to twenty years old. She meant everything to me. When as a teenager I adopted her I had plenty of issues with humans I had yet to resolve. I have never really been a people person and tended to view humans as a nuisance at best and the enemy at worst. There were reasons for this. The family I was brought up in wasn't the easiest of spaces in which a young person could grow. Also as a child I had to contend with the same social pressures that all girls had to put up with at the time. Sexism and classism were rife. Men thought it was okay to touch young girls in passing. They would grab your bottom or breast. They would gawp at your body, leer and make comments that were highly sexual and inappropriate to say to young females. Walking down the street as a ten year old was to have your body and gender constantly commented on, discussed and abused. I grew up thinking that all men were paedophiles although I didn't know the word. That all men thought they had access to your body to stare at, evaluate and deride. This was very difficult for me to cope with emotionally as a young girl and my response was to acquire a very bad attitude towards men and boys indeed. By the time I was a teenager I had got into a few fights. If I was walking along the street and a man commented on my breasts with the usual popular abuse of the time "Look at the tits on that" more often than not I would get into an argument with him. Sometimes it lead to fights. If I pulled someone up about his behaviour I would sometimes get attacked. My response was to go along to a local community centre and learn some karate. Practicing the bits I could manage with a friend I once put my leg through a plate glass door when I misjudged his expertise at dodging my kicks. Chris who prefers to avoid conflict would never respond if he heard anyone insult me, so he would end up watching on the sidelines while I traded insults with some local low life on the pavements where we lived.

In the Eighties at the height of the women's movement in Britain there was plenty of critical theory around to give me pause for thought about how men treated women. It was the time of multiple murders of working class women in the north of England by a man who claimed to have mental health problems. Women had little economic power and if they were economically dependant on men often put up with terrible physical and emotional violence because they had no financial backup if they needed to leave. I had married briefly as a teenager to a man who was prepared to be violent to try to dominate me. When I took him to court to try to get him out of our jointly owned house the judge told me to go home and make up with him. He was let off completely and I had to go on living in the same house as him for a while. I left him not long afterwards but the judges advice was indicative of the prevailing ethos towards the violence women were expected to put up with at the time.

I began to read lots of theory from women's movement feminist writers and decided to call myself a political lesbian. This was a concept popular with certain groups of women at the time that foregrounded what was known as seperatism. This was a concept that revolved around women cutting men and male influence out of their lives as much as possible. There should be no engagement with men either financially or personally. Any fraternisation was seen as colluding with patriarchal systems. I wanted to be as independent of men as possible. The political lesbian theory was roughly that if you wanted to change the violence and unfairness of a patriarchal systems treatment of women you had to withdraw as much labour and contact from those male systems as possible. Give all your energy to other women. Live with them. Support them. Interact with them economically and sleep with them. Some feminists had to learn to enjoy the last part of this implied directive. I naturally gravitated towards women anyway, so for me this was all good. I shaved all my hair off so as not to attract any male attention and bought myself some vegan doc martens, I bought mens clothes from charity shops, suits with big shoulders that looked like gangster clothes, in honour of my working class hero of the time, the actor James Cagney, and I kept up my trousers with wide braces. I probably looked like a cartoon character from a comic strip but the gay women I met seemed to enjoy me so I embarked on a period of my life when I tried to ignore and bypass the existence of men. This must have been awkward for Chris because we still shared a house out of financial expediency as there weren't any other lesbian seperatists in Bridgwater. There were times though when I imported a new woman friend from another County who also called herself a political lesbian, or other seperatists who refused to speak to men at all. So Chris would be in our shared house on the settee reading and in would come another stroppy dyke. This must have made life quite bewildering for Chris who would offer to make them tea and get ignored. Years later in Glastonbury he met an ex seperatist who had given him the cold shoulder years before and she apologised to him. I think he was underwhelmed. None the less I met some fabulous lesbian women and did lots of campaigning with them. I learned a lot and was encouraged in my vegan beliefs.

For various reasons I was still unenamoured of the human race as a whole, so when I adopted Floyd I appreciated her company and intelligence without my distaste of people getting in the way of a friendship. She was company without hassle and I had many years of relaxing companionship with her. Many of the lesbian women I went out with had adopted rescue dogs and would often bring animals with them when they came to stay with us. Floyd, Bramble and I would show them our favourite walks and we would spend the early mornings or summer afternoons ambling along country lanes along the outskirts of Bridgwater. Many of these lanes still exist today and in spring the same snowdrops and mauve violets still bloom under the hedges next to wild daffodils, bluebells and red and white campion.

Like Bramble, Floyd enjoyed vibrant good health. We spent long days out in the fields with picnics. I would find a tree stump to sit on and throw balls for the two dogs. There were mushrooms and fungus to pick quite often. One afternoon I found a large so called beefsteak fungus growing on a tree trunk and I cut it off and took it home to fry with herbs and onions. Some of the local fields were managed without pesticide and I have wonderful memories of walking waist high in wild flowers and herbs in these green spaces with the dogs. Photographs I have at home attest to the many places Floyd, Bramble and I enjoyed all year round. One of my favourite places to take them was Dunster deer park. Dunster nestles on the edge of Exmoor off the A39. It has a beautiful castle and watermill and in the summer is thronged with tourists. If you go through the village behind the castle there is a path that goes over a pack horse bridge. It takes you over a clear, wide stream that leads up into the hills. With my painful back and increasing mobility problems it would often take some time to get up to the deer park with frequent stops where the dogs would sniff around following the scent of wildlife and chewing sticks.

Eventually we would get to the open moorland where raptors glide overhead on the thermals and the sun blasts down on the bare, dry land. Apart from the occasional horse rider travelling past we would be on our own in the quiet space with just the bird calls and the cooling breeze for company. Floyd was an amazing companion with an eye for detail. Even in those days I may have had symptoms of the Sjorgens syndrome that was later to make itself felt so much in my life. Back then I was prone to lose things, often house keys. At the deer park one day I lost everything from my pockets and had to retrace my steps later that day with Floyd. She found everything that had fallen out of my pocket, including a solitary house key amongst all the ferns and greenery. Floyd was an instinctive and empathic companion, her intelligence was razor sharp and she got the measure of me quickly in her knowing way. Her quiet and thoughtful company became a great pleasure in my life. We became inseparable. Where I was Floyd was. This could make life tricky. There are places that dogs aren't allowed and at times I stopped going to shops and even friends houses where dogs were not welcome. A favourite cafe in Glastonbury changed hands. Before that Floyd had been accepted inside the building while we ate but the new owners would not allow her to stay. I left the food I'd ordered uneaten and we never went back to dine there again. I thought that the places that banned dogs before they were legally obliged to were practicing a kind of apartheid. If my dogs couldn't go there I wouldn't patronise it or visit there myself.

Everything revolved around the dogs. This made them confident and secure creatures. They were never hit or treated unkindly. As a result I had two relaxed and healthy dogs. That's if you don't count Brambles fiery temperament but then being assertive and barking a lot was one of her ways of relaxing. Bramble was always looking for fights or bundles as we used to call her occasional skirmishes in the park. We never encouraged this and went out of our way to prevent it by keeping her lead on near dogs she didn't know. Sometimes with heavy hearts we had to put a muzzle on her briefly when walking to destinations through the crowded park. That didn't stop her looking very pleased and interested if she saw other dogs in the park engaged in a disagreement. Floyd was the opposite and avoided conflict at all costs. If another dog became interested in her she would say hello politely with a quick muzzle sniff and then walk away. Her vet said she would make a good Surgery dog helping anxious animals to relax in his waiting room.

Neither Bramble nor Floyd got ill very much, as they aged they both became a little arthritic but this was very late on in life and for the most part they remained healthy and strong. Due to their organic diet and constant exercise they developed muscled shoulders and agile bodies. At one point in their youths they spent a lot of time managing to climb certain trees. On one walk with a girlfriend of the time they disappeared momentarily and my friend was astounded when she looked up to see them grinning down from the tree canopy above her. Floyd enjoyed swimming. In the Hamp fields there is a stream that borders some public space, Floyd loved to wade into it in the summer when it was full of stickleback fish and glittering blue dragonflies. She would stand in the cool stream on a hot day and watch the insects flitting around in the afternoon sun. I have so many memories of bright days with her in the Somerset countryside where first she and I and then with Bramble joining us spent time outside. Alone in the fields I could sit and watch the world go by while the dogs would chase balls or chew sticks.
Floyd remained vibrantly healthy and happy for most of her life. We had so many lovely times together and even now when she has been gone for so many years I can still remember those afternoons with her as if they just happened yesterday.

When illness eventually struck Floyd I felt like I had been punched in the stomach. I had noticed a small lump on her underside whilst grooming her. The vet said it was a fatty lump and probably nothing to worry about but that I should keep an eye on it. I monitored it and for some time it remained the same size. After a while another lump grew next to it, we went back to have it examined by the vet. This time it was news that made me feel sick inside. "I think it's cancer" the vet said quietly. "It may not grow quickly, but we could take it out". Chris and I thought about it. We didn't want Floyds cancer to spread. Sick with worry I gave the vet permission to operate. Waiting for the surgery to finish so we could get round to the vets to pick her up was tense. I phoned the vets receptionist and although it was probably only a minute or two I waited on the phone it seemed to take forever until the nurse came back with an answer. The operation was a success in that the lump had been removed and Floyd had come round from the anaesthetic, Chris and I could pick her up in a few hours. We called a black London taxi which had enough space in the back to put her big whicker dog basket. She was still groggy from the operation when we picked her up. I had never seen a dog who had just come out of surgery before and I was aghast to see the wound in her flesh with white thread stitches holding it closed and blood still leaking out from the wound. We took her home carefully as she was still groggy, Bramble was allowed to see her very briefly so she knew what was going on but we kept her lead on in case she tried to attack her recumbent companion. Floyd was then kept seperate from Bramble for a few days in case her liveliness caused Floyd any distress. Slowly she began to recover. We visited the vet twice more. I was worried because blood kept seeping from her wound and on the second occasion to have the stitches removed. The vet told us frankly that the cancer might return but that she should be okay for at least a few months.

I was grateful for this extension to her life, but it also made me realize that after all these years with my beautiful friend that the time for her to die was fast approaching. Not immediately but in the not too distant future. This was very hard to take in. Floyd had been my constant companion and as much as I loved Bramble Floyd was the first dog I had cared for. We had a very special bond. After years in each others company I felt we had something akin to telepathy. Maybe it was custom. The endless cycle of eat, sleep and live your life. Maybe we had grown so used to one another that we could both predict the others intention or next move. Chris and I had continued to share homes although he worked so many hours that when he wasn't walking the dog I barely saw him. Although I visited family and friends it was with the dogs I spent the bulk of my free time and it was to Floyd in particular that I felt most close. Losing Floyd would mean losing my closest friend. It is impossible to catalogue all the things I lost when she eventually closed her eyes for the last time. In the meantime after her operation to remove the cancerous lump we would have unbeknown to us at the time one more year to show friendship and love to each other before Floyd would be put to sleep forever.

We had moved to another crummy terrace by then. I had managed to get onto an access course to catch up on missed education and was in my first year at university as a mature student. I was working full time evenings three or four days a week as a residential social worker planning activities for adults with autism. The night shifts fitted in with my study at the University of the West of England where I was reading a degree that included Women's studies, English literature and Philosophy.

At that period of time my life was very busy, I could leave the dogs with Chris while I worked evenings knowing they would be in safe hands and well cared for. In the day time I had to board Floyd out on one occasion while I drove to university in Bristol. Floyd did not appreciate being boarded even for a few hours. After a six hour stint in kennels she was very angry with me when I returned to collect her. For the first of only two times in her life she came up to me straight out of the kennel and barked in my face. After we got into our creaky old car she continued barking. For a full fifteen minutes I got the telling off of my life. It was very clear Floyd did not appreciate being locked up in a run next to other dogs whose selfish owners had disappeared on holiday. The kennel man said she had been silent with her back turned to him all day. She was saving her annoyance for when she caught up with me. Having been treated as an equal all her life I imagine Floyd could not quite work out who the kennel man thought he was locking her in a run with no armchair and no room service. It was an experience that made her so angry that she raved at me all the way home in the car. Putting her in a kennel, even briefly was something I would never do again. I apologised humbly but my haughty black and white companion turned her muzzle away from me to let me know there would be serious consequences for our *entente cordiale* if I ever repeated this mistake.

Bramble on the other hand, seemed to have been delighted in her separate run to be able to prance about barking abuse at the top of her voice with her ruff stood up menacing other dogs through the mesh of the run. Bramble had barked so much that she lost her voice for two days. When we took her back to board occasionally she would tug on her lead to get into the kennels and once in her run she would turn her back on us and concentrate on some serious barking.

The year after her operation passed quickly for Floyd and I. We spent lots of time in the nearby park watching the world go by. Bright days of summer enjoying the soft grass of the park or cuddled up under the giant chestnut trees that shade its paths. Being under them was like being in natures cathedral with the massive gnarled trunks leading up to huge branches covered in bright green leaves reaching up to the sky, light dappled between the foliage with the clouds behind. It is vivid memories like these that frame my remembrance of the last days I was to have with her. Floyds arthritis became more apparent and a growth appeared right on her breast, we kept an eye on it but it grew until it started to look lumpy and more obviously like a cancer. We canvassed the vet for his opinion. He said he did not think another operation would help. At twenty years old he didn't know if she would survive the anesthetic and he felt that the cancer might have spread inside her. He said the time was approaching when we would have to put her to sleep. This was an impossible thought for me to countenance, I could not process it in my head. Floyd was the friend I loved most in the world. I would have given my life for her in an instant if it would have helped. Of course nothing was going to help. Floyd was dying of cancer and the vet said we would need to put her down. Coming to that decision was agony. We had to say goodbye but It was something I could not do. Chris and I were paralysed by 'what if's'. What if the vet was wrong and another operation would help? What if we left it for a while to see how it went? Maybe we should stop vacillating and take her to the vets that afternoon and get it over and done with. In the end I could do none of these things. We took her to the vet for painkillers and another examination, we nursed her day and night. One person would stay with her while the other drove to uni. we spent our every waking minute with her in the last few days of her life. My vet was very firm with me. He said if we didn't let him kill her soon she would start to suffer. I did not want that but something was missing in my head. I could not willingly agree to euthanase her. I was desperate for a solution to her problems but I didn't know where to turn. I remember that time in our lives as unrelenting and unbearable stress.

Floyd spent her time sleeping in her basket or by the front door under which a breeze came to keep her cool. One evening uncharacteristically I went to the pub for a short break from the unrelenting pressure of the decision I could not make. A neighbour was there with his black and white collie, I told him about my difficulty in having my dog killed to save her from the pain of cancer. I stayed for about fifteen minutes, When I got home

Chris was sat with Floyd on the floor, her head was resting on his legs. When I walked into the room he got up to go to the kitchen. Floyd came up to me and as I bent down to speak to her, for the second time in her whole life, she barked loudly and directly into my face. I believe she was asking me to kill her. She knew her time was up. I lay down on the floor next to her whilst she got comfy on her blanket and I rested my cheek on hers. "I know what you're saying Floyd" I told her "But I can't kill you, I love you too much". As she fell asleep in the breeze from under the door I lay next to her and wept bitter tears because my friend was dying and there was nothing I could do to help her regain her health or live a few months more. She needed me to put an end to her life before her suffering increased and, useless creature that I felt I was, I did not think that I would be able to.

The solution presented itself. I had always been a believer in alternative therapies. If Floyds usual vet couldn't help my ailing friend maybe I should go somewhere else. I searched through the yellow pages until I found a homeopathic vet on the Somerset levels. Floyd and I drove there in my old Sierra estate. As the lanes passed the car windows in the early throes of spring, I was conscious of the vivid colours of the surrounding landscape. The vibrant blue sky and sparkling water in the ditches. Catkins appearing on the myriad willows that lined the road. Passing the nature reserve I noticed that birds whose names I didn't know, had landed in the fields adding to the magic of this special place. Everything outside the car seemed so bright and hopeful as I drove along to the homeopathic vet. Floyd was laying along the length of the back seat. My careful driving allowed her to sleep. I remembered the times we had driven along this road for a day out in Glastonbury when dogs were still allowed in what was then an entirely vegan cafe. Friends and I would have lunch and Floyd would lie under the table sleeping off a ramble on the levels. Sometimes we would attend a vegan event with Bramble and the two dogs would wait at the head of the food queue mugging passing vegans with their canine charm until each one felt obliged to hand over a small piece of their animal free dinner to the charming canine assailants.

This time as we drove through the streets of Glastonbury the town seemed strangely quiet. A few colourfully dressed women were ambling along in the pale sunshine. Outside one shop were bunches of spring flowers in purple and yellow. Travellers with dogs on bits of rope were sitting with cans of special brew on the bench outside the church. We passed by all these familiar sights as usual but today we were not part of the picture. I felt like I was negotiating my way through a fairy tale or a particularly unpleasant dream. If only I could find the secret to some mystical conundrum the evil dilemma would recede and Floyds renewed vigour would be my prize. This fantasy acted as distraction while I drove towards the vets.

As we got there I felt a mixture of hope and terror. My stomach churned with acid in anticipation of words I could not bear to hear. I parked the car outside the building and helped Floyd gently out of it. She walked slowly and carefully like an animal that is being led to the slaughter. "It's alright Floyd" I told her "This is a new vet. We'll see if he can help". We didn't have to wait long in the reception area, when I got into the vets surgery. He could see the state we were both in. Floyd was scared and I was distraught. I tried to relate to him all the details of her illness and my inability to give her other vet the permission he needed to put her to death. I told him how torn I felt and asked him if there was anything he could do for her. He sat on the edge of the table looking at Floyd. She was laying quietly on the floor. To a stranger I suppose he saw a very old creature on her way out. Her fur was still jet black and thick contrasting the white tips on her paws. Her muzzle had turned to silver and white. Her venerable age seemed to glisten before me as I joined him in quietly regarding her. "What is it you need from me?" he asked. I couldn't speak and I started to cry silently. Hot, salty tears coursed down my face and ran into the neck of my T shirt. "I want her to have a natural death" I said "In her sleep with no pain, I can't seem to do any more to help her." He replied "I have a pill I could give you, take it home and give it to her tonight". I have forgotten what this pill was called but bizarrely I remember he had a notice on his wall saying do not give whatever this pill was in the case of one of Floyds symptoms. I was not thinking straight and by now my inability to deal with the situation emotionally had left me in total shutdown. Floyd could not wait for me to get my act together any longer. Still I could not give permission for the vet to kill her.

I drove slowly home through the country lanes. In truth I had become a virtual zombie. When we arrived home we had a slow walk in the park and I decided I wouldn't go upstairs to bed. I would stay on the ground floor with Floyd. Chris and Bramble went upstairs to sleep in Brambles room so as not to disturb us. I tried pointlessly to give Floyd a vitamin tablet. She refused to open her mouth so let it drop to the floor. She looked straight into my eyes and then she lay down on the bed that Chris usually slept in at the downstairs front of the house. I lay next to her and remembered the vets tablet, I took it out of the small white envelope it was in. I had forgotten what it was and this time Floyd didn't seem to mind when I put it in her mouth. As I lay next to her stroking her back I talked to her. Years before she'd had a doggy friend called Jack who had died from cancer. At the time I had tried to explain his death to her. This night I told her "Floyd, you are dying like Jack". She lay still for a few minutes then she called out to me. A call I had not heard before which turned out to be the last sound she ever made. The vets tablet, whatever it was, had done its job. I honestly hadn't realised what it was for. Floyd had died on the bed lying next to me from the drug given to me by the homeopathic vet. Despite all my reluctance and inability to act this man had given us a solution to our terminal dilemma, she had eaten the tablet and now she was gone.

Suddenly her body was limp and she started to slide down the bed. I panicked irrationally, because nothing could hurt her now. I shouted for Chris and together we pulled Floyd back onto the bed. Chris, who had been upstairs sleeping, told me Bramble had woken him and walked in a circle to the door. It was her way of saying she knew Floyd was gone. We lay Floyd on the middle of the bed and took turns looking at her unmoving body. I held her paw and told her quietly about all the things she had meant in my life. She had been there since I was a defensive, angry teenager, right through to my growing into an adult and beyond. She was the only creature on the planet I felt had an accurate measure of me. Dogs watch you and smell your happiness and fear. This beautiful old collie had lived her life with passion and intelligence and was an entirely unique creature. She wasn't bothered about humans in general but was loving and generous of giving her time to me. Chris and I took turns talking to her. We stayed with her, shell shocked for two days on and off, covering her with a blanket to keep her body cool. Day turned to night then day and night again. I told Chris. "I can't bear to leave her, even though I know she's gone." As Floyd was drifting into death I had been holding her paw while speaking to her. She had died with one ear up listening to me speak. Even in death she had given me her whole attention. Everything I had and had ever been had been geared to her comfort for the love of her.

I couldn't move on the days after her death and I couldn't bear to have her burnt or buried. At the time we were renting a house but I had ambitions to move somewhere with a proper garden. Chris, who knew I was a fan of fairy tales came up with a solution, He said "we could put her in a freezer until one day when you have a garden where you can bury her. Right away I felt more calm. If she went into a freezer I wouldn't have to bury her immediately and I could look at her occasionally so I wouldn't forget her face. This was one of the things that had been worrying me. There is no correct way to grieve. No map. No signpost. This was the death of the first dog I had the privilege to care for and to me it had huge importance. We bought a chest freezer and lined it with comfy blankets, Chris gently lifted Floyd inside. Her ear was still sticking up where she had been listening to me when she died. We switched the freezer on and put her into it with her beloved yellow tennis ball between her front paws. I put a little satin cushion next to her and every year I would put fresh flowers on it on the anniversary of her death. She had died in March so I pick spring flowers for her every year. When someone on the radio was interviewing me about Floyd because of her unusual resting place asked me if this was a strange state of affairs I said "Yes I suppose so but I have heard some people put dead animals in freezers and then eat them, to me this seems more strange". I continued to talk to Floyd on and off and cover her in flowers. I never did let go of her and while there is breath in my body I never will. When my time comes to shuffle off this mortal coil I hope I can be put on the ground next to all of my beautiful, gentle canine friends. With Floyd laying by my side in death as she always did in life.

Mourning Floyd

Chapter Six.

Bramble Has an Accident.

Struggling to survive had taken up most of my time as a young adult on poverty wages and I was always too busy to go to an evening class. Now in my thirties something called an Access course had arrived at the local college. You could apply for it with no qualifications and if you passed it you could go on to university. I applied for a place while sharing a house with Chris and another vegan called Reg. Initially only Reg and I applied, Chris said he didn't have the confidence. From a glance around at interview time I knew the college had some vegan food in the cafe. Reg and I lured Chris in with a promise of lunch. By the time he'd eaten veggie burger, chips and beans and a fourth cup of tea from the vending machine Chris was full of confidence and his fear of college had gone. He could see that most of the pupils were young and busy but there were a good few older people about, some of whom he knew. By the end of lunch we had talked Chris into applying for an Access course. We were all going to college. The three musketeers.

Wellington road is a stones throw from Bridgwater college and the Access course was part time. It would take up our mornings but the dogs could walk before we went and again after lunch. We could evolve a routine to fit in with everyone.

I had always enjoyed reading and studying. It was a dream of mine to go to university. When I left school in the seventies I had gone to the careers service and asked how people go about getting to Art college, the careers officer said there wasn't a local one and my parents didn't know how to find out where the college was. "Anyway" said mum "We could never afford bus fares". Despite a lack of formal education I had been a voracious reader and had some of my prose and poetry published in women's magazines. I'd written some stuff about animal rights which was published in a political journal, so I was confident that all would be well. Neither Reg or Chris had been to college but were keen to give it a go and we settled into the routine of study.

All the pupils on our Access course were adult learners and most of our tutors were the same age as us. The work was interesting and the subjects varied including English, Sociology and Psychology. Some of the tutors were especially enthusiastic about their subjects and I came away with a passion for Thomas Hardy and plenty of food for thought.

Bramble and Floyd were getting older but were still vigorous and strong. Confident they could be looked after still Chris, Reg and I applied for university. Life was looking up at last. We drove up to our interviews at the University of the West of England in my old red van and waited nervously in a corridor. An hour later after our various interviews we had a result. Chris and I were accepted, but Reg had not been invited on a course. A few weeks later we were heading up to Bristol every morning. With varying time tables the dogs could come with us and be cared for by one if us, while the other sat in a lecture. Reg came for the ride and would spend his time in town.

The course Chris and I did included a mixed major in English and Women's studies, with a dash of philosophy. Fed up with bailiffs, drunks and rogue landladies it was a relief to sit in the airy buildings with stained glass windows and consider the narratives of varying moral and spiritual codes.

There weren't many visible vegans at Uni and the students union bar didn't really cater for us, except for potatoes. Also the bar was always full of smoke. We took our own food and ate it in the van, where we could enjoy the company of Floyd and Bramble, just back from a city walk. If it was my turn to look after them I would drive to the waterside and they could amble along watching the boats and swans.

Time passed quickly at Uni. As well as study and essays I'd had to find a flexible job. To pay our fees we'd had to get student loans and we both had to buy dog food, petrol and pay bills. Chris and I found jobs working for a local charity and we started shifts there from 2p.m till 10. I became a residential social worker working with adults with Autistic Spectrum Disorder. As Chris worked different hours to me we could still both care for the dogs.

During my time working with Adults with autism I learnt a lot about myself, other people and the phenomena of projection. Working with adults with autism you very quickly learn what it is like to be in communication with people who do not give back what you expect emotionally and whose perception of what you take for granted is very different from your own.

After I'd been at my place of work for a while as a bank worker I was taken on as permanent staff and could work in my favourite spot. A house with people displaying challenging behavior. At first I was a little alarmed about what sort of behavior I would meet but with training and support both Chris and I learnt to deal with any challenges and very much enjoyed our time in our jobs.

Being at Uni full time and working on shifts meant any other time left was spent on rota caring for the dogs. There were three of us there to care for them but they were mostly dealt with by myself and Chris. Reg tended to read a lot or was endlessly fixing gadgets or working on his bike. While Chris trundled round St. Mathews field or the Hamp fields behind with the dogs. Reg would sit by the stream and sketch rural scenes in oil pastels.

The first two years at Uni passed in a blur of work. Partly with the care work and often with long essays. I had dropped the women's studies after the first year to concentrate on the English and I was reading about ideas I hadn't come across before. Some of the recommended books were challenging. I remember standing in a corridor waiting for a lecture to start, wondering how I was going to cope emotionally with reading Foucaults 'Discipline and Punish' full of descriptions of murder and torture. The English critical theory was engaging and I enjoyed reading Derrida among others. Some authors like Terry Eagleton, I found a little dry. With the disparate reading at Uni and the perceptions gained in my job I thought I might go on to further study if I could fit it in with the dogs.

Just after my second year at Uni. Floyd died. It was a huge blow and hard to bear, but essays still needed to be handed in and I still had to work. I drove to Bristol and spent time with Bramble. All the time I wasn't studying I spent thinking of Floyd.

Life carried on inexorably. I kept my memories of my beloved dog alive by remembering times we shared. Chris and I could talk about her and even the normally unemotional Reg said he was sorry that she'd gone. Around the same time our landlady in Wellington road had got married and wanted to sell our rented house. We still had Bramble, Sally and now Stan and Dreadlock, so it was hard to find another property to rent due to the unwillingness of landlords to allow dogs in their rented houses.

After trying without luck to find somewhere to live we spoke to the local paper, I explained that my dog had died and was being kept in a freezer. We needed a rental quickly but nowhere to live transpired. The story did make the nationals though and reporters wrote about Bramble and came to take her picture. One magazine did a story which paid for some dog food. Eventually just before we were due to leave the small terrace a neighbour agreed to rent us his house. It was two doors away from our current house so no need for a removal van. Bramble, Sam, Sally and Dreadlock found it odd walking out of one house straight into another but it was a relief to get away from the neighbour who had complained about me singing Janis Joplin songs in the bath.

Around the time Chris and I finished our second year at Uni Reg moved back to the north of the country where his parents lived. After his application to study had been unsuccessful he seemed at a bit of a loss what to do with his life and as Chris and I were going to be busy and not much company it made sense for Reg to get on with his life elsewhere. We saw him off on the coach bound for Manchester with his pushbike in the luggage hold at the back. Now it was just us, the dogs and hopefully the future.

Bramble had begun to slow up during this time. She remained healthy and happy to exercise but she was changing. Sometimes she would come out of a room, stand around, then go back in again looking very much like someone who had forgotten what they had come out for. When walking with Bramble and Sally we would take Sallys lead off so that she could walk at her own pace because Bramble couldn't keep up and we didn't want to rush her.

When we moved house we gave Bramble and Sally space in the downstairs front room and we kept Dreadlock in the back. Although he would have been very gentle with the old ladies, Dreadlock was a bit like an articulated lorry when he turned round in the small house, his huge blonde tail had been known to sweep the cups off the coffee table. Bramble would have to be kept out of his way.

Despite sally being quite old when I took her on she was still way younger than her ancient companion. Nonetheless the two became good friends and spent all their time in each others company. I think their favourite day was Sunday due to their beach walk at Burnham on sea. Although Sally walked much faster than Bramble she would content herself with running up and down the beach with huge sticks, while Bramble ambled sedately at my side. If Chris was with us he would throw sticks in the sea for Sally to swim out and fetch in case she got bored waiting for Bramble.

Across the water from Burnham beach lie the towering nuclear reactors of Hinkley point. Whilst watching the most beautiful sunsets on the horizon it is hard to ignore these alien structures from an industry that has been the subject of so much controversy over the years. Much of Burnham beach is closed to dogs during the tourist season, so Bramble and Sally would have to be driven to the outskirts of the town before they could walk on the sand. On the way home Bramble would fall asleep as we drove down the dual carriageway to home, while Sally stood with her shoulder to the car door and her head out of the window where she would bark loudly on hearing the words 'hedges' or 'plants'.

Stans favourite walk was I believe, the forest at Wind down. Not a dog who enjoyed the town, he seemed to feel more comfortable walking quietly like Brambles shadow in the woodland. Wind down is fairly deserted much of the time, so it was here that Chris took gentle anxious Stan for most of his afternoon strolls. Here at the advent of evening if walking quietly they could see small herds of deer crossing the winding paths, and sometimes a fox who was abroad at the same time each day looking for food. If a vixen had cubs to feed they might find a rabbits head severed from her body just left on the path.

One afternoon when Bramble, Sally and I were returning from a visit to the river in Bridgwater Bramble had a terrible accident. At the end of their walk the old ladies liked to stand on a run of steps by the river and look down on the scene a few feet below them. Bramble liked to pretend, I think that she was the owner of all she surveyed. We had a standing joke, Chris or I would sing to her "You're the king of the castle" as she looked down on us. This day as Bramble was contemplating her domain Sally ran down the steps unexpectedly and headed back for the car. As it was parked near a busy road I ran after her and grabbed her to put her lead on. When I went back for Bramble twenty seconds later there was no sign of her on top of the steps where she had been only moments before. Something white on the concrete next to the steps caught my eye. It was Bramble. She had fallen off of her vantage point to the unforgiving floor below. It was a height of about six feet. She was laying on the path very still, not making a sound. Looking at her I got a terrible feeling of doom in the pit of my stomach. For a minute I thought she was dead.

I rushed over to her and looked down into her open brown eyes, she was still breathing and as I approached she let out a little cry. Instinctively I gathered her into my arms and somehow, despite my chronic back problems I managed to get her into the car. Leaving Sally in the front seat I got Bramble into the vets where her Scots vet, Andy looked at her "she's paralyzed down one side" he said "Peraplegic, I don't think she'll walk again. You'll have to put her down". The familiar sinking feeling I get whenever any of my dogs are seriously ill flooded through me. I had taken extreme care of Bramble all of her life. I had grown organic veg for her, invented a special diet and dedicated virtually my entire life to the comfort of her and the other dogs who lived in my home. I was in shock that a few seconds distraction with Sally meant that I was not with her when she needed me. I blamed myself for her fall and felt I was a very stupid woman.

Bramble lay on the vets table very still. The vet gave her anti-inflammatory injection and asked what I wanted to do. I said it was too early to decide there and then and I needed time to research her condition. Despite his belief that she probably wouldn't walk again I accepted his suggestion to give her painkillers and I left the surgery to research paraplegia. Chris who had been called out of work gently took Bramble home on a stiff board and when she was settled safely into her room, I rang a friend who is a nurse of humans and she told me to visit her so I could use her computer. I looked up paralysis in dogs. There wasn't a great deal of information but one text on the net was from someone who had used hydrotherapy to facilitate recovery from similar injury in a person. I rang the vet back and asked if they knew anywhere that did hydrotherapy for canines. Miracle of miracles there was a pool dedicated to dogs only and it was just a few miles from where we lived. Two days after her fall we gently drove Bramble there in the car on her stiff board. After negotiating the twisting lanes near Cannington we found a cottage with a sign, 'Magic's pool for dogs'.

The owner and therapist is an ex Broadmoor nurse and dog enthusiast called Pam. Chris and I were in bits emotionally when we took Bramble there for the first time. Pam was very reassuring that everything would be okay. She spoke to Bramble and carefully put a little red life jacket on her. Bramble looked anxious but didn't move to object. Chris was told to put on a wetsuit like the one Pam was wearing and very slowly he and she lifted Bramble into the large, round pool.

Bramble was never a fan of water and it's fair to say she looked quite frightened but I think she was so shocked and tired by her accident that she had no energy to demur. Pam held Bramble around her side and supported her between her front paws so her head stayed out of the water and she told Chris to hold her legs at the Back and move them with a paddling motion in. This was to allow her muscles to be worked so they didn't atrophy without any effort or strain on the dog. Usually Pam's canine clients would have an hour in the pool strengthening their legs to heal any injuries, but for her first time Chris and I felt half an hour would be enough. Pam and Chris lifted Bramble out of the water and Pam placed her on a thick white towel and began to gently rub her dry. After getting the worst of the water off she took out a hairdryer to finish the job. For the first time that day Bramble made her opinion known and she lunged at Pam with her long pointed teeth. Pam seemed adept at dodging nips and said " I don't blame you for wanting to bite Bramble. You must be in a lot of pain". Chris put his hand in the way of Brambles teeth, while Pam put some rose water or similar, on our very grumpy friend and cut a small piece of Brambles fur off. This she put into a bag then gave us a small crystal. She said "This will help with healing, don't worry she'll get better, I promise" I shed a few tears while she talked to us because she was giving us hope that Bramble would recover in contrast to the more grim prognosis of the vet. Pam also said she did Reiki and would also use this to facilitate Brambles recovery. Chris then picked Bramble up as if she were made or fragile glass and loaded her into the car. Pam said we would see a definite improvement in a month. We really wanted to believe her.

The next session we took Bramble for a few days later produced startling results. After another half an hour of being supported in the water by Pam and Chris and having her legs carefully moved, Bramble walked out of her second therapy session. It was just from the pool house to the car, about ten feet and she was a little wobbly, but walk she did. We were ecstatic and could barely believe it. After one hour of hydrotherapy over two weeks Bramble had taken her first steps again. Pam's prediction was coming true. I put my arms around Pam and gave her a giant hug "Thank you so much" I said "You're a life saver". Then we drove Bramble home and tucked her up in her warm bed.

After our third session of hydro Pam gave us a dog trolley that we could strap Bramble in to assist her walking, but she didn't like so we took it back. It was a task of constant care and vigilance rehabilitating the elderly dog. Chris would have to pick her up carefully and hold her outside in the kerb for her wees. She still couldn't stand up for long on her own, she could walk a few steps but then she would falter. We continued with the hydrotherapy and she made improvements every week. We became used to the drive towards Stogursey to magic's pool on Tuesday mornings. Chris altered his working hours so he could be there every week. He got used to feeling silly in his tight black wet suit and was happy to wield a net in the water to pick up any floating faeces that Bramble would do. Pam was a mine of information on dog care from herbal remedies to the characteristics of different breeds and she told us that her pool had been named after her munsterlander friend 'Magic' after the dogs death. It's fair to say I don't think Bramble ever enjoyed her hydrotherapy and we always limited it to half an hour a week so she wouldn't get too tired because at the time she was geriatric in the extreme. There's no doubt though that it restored her mobility to her one hundred percent. After a few sessions she actually skipped out of the pool room like a puppy and when her hydro finished I can honestly say her mobility was better than it had been before the accident.

Prior to her fall, like many old dogs, she had a touch of arthritis and could be a bit stiff on waking. As the day progressed she would loosen up a bit. After her hydro sessions she was much more flexible and fluid in her movements. On one occasion while she and Sally were walking on Burnham beach I said to Chris "Do you think she is happy?" Bramble gave a little dance in the manner that young lambs move. We took this as a definite "Yes". Thanks to Pam Bramble regained full mobility and her movement improved no end. From this I learnt there is often something you can do to improve a dire situation. We could have given up on her after she fell but that would have been the easy situation. Apart from her temporary paralysis on one side she was a game old girl and tough after living a long and rich life. The local and regional press were interested in Brambles hydrotherapy and a television crew came down to Pam's pool to film one of her sessions. We wanted to show people that even when something appears to be your darkest hour there is often something you can do to turn the situation around.

Pam put photos of Bramble on her leaflet advertising the pool and cut out a picture from the press of Bramble and stuck it on her wall. Long after Bramble had died when we visited the pool with another dog, Brambles picture was still there proudly in its place among the photos of all the other dogs Pam had helped to recover. It was strange to be back there in the humid atmosphere of the place that meant so much to us when Bramble was alive. I will always be grateful to Pam who gave us hope when everything seemed bleak. Truly something magical happened for Bramble in Magic's pool for dogs.

Later when Chris heard of another dog that had been in a terrible accident he spoke to the carer who was going to put the collie down and she handed her care over to Pam. This dog also made a full recovery.

Chapter Seven.

Respecting Dogs.

Managing a dog for longevity will require you to think about animals in unfamiliar ways. It is often human attitudes to dogs that cause many of them to die or be killed years earlier than they would otherwise live to.

Often if animals are old or ill people will take the lethal option and have them killed rather than provide the care they would give if they were dealing with a human casualty. So many healthy dogs are killed today that people are less likely to keep a dog alive that has a manageable illness or has broken a limb for example. Conditions that would be viewed as treatable in human patients are often used as a reason to kill domesticated dogs or cats. So called euthenasia by vets then is one reason animals lives may be cut short. The agreement between carers and vets is essentially contract killing. If a dog is suffering and unlikely to recover this may be seen as kind. Many times a carer can't be bothered to engage in lengthy care so an animal is killed.

After untimely, arranged demise stress is another major reason dogs die earlier than necessary. Apart from accidental matings all other dogs will have been deliberately bred. Most breeders are in it for the money, they are selling souls. Breeders may be people who run their business from home on a small scale, or they may be running the appalling puppy mills that are often uncovered by covert investigation. Either way they are churning out lives for money. Puppy mills breed dogs in horrific conditions. They are dirty and overcrowded, exploiting the breeding bitches in their care. These females are relentlessly used until they are too old and ill. They are then discarded or killed, occasionally they end up in shelters. Litters bred from these exhausted creatures may be born diseased. The smaller breeder still exploits animals and for every puppy bought from a small breeder American welfare organization Peta says a dog in a shelter dies because that potential home has been lost and another healthy animal will be killed. Small breeders are also using the same bitches to churn out puppies repeatedly. Every time they give birth the offspring of these bitches will be torn away from their mothers causing depression and distress. In my opinion the same distress that human mammals feel when their children are stolen, all creatures will protect their young. Bitches used for repeated breeding will lack nutrients and vigor, which will impact on puppy health. For these puppies stress begins even before they are born as they grow inside their ailing mothers.

Puppies that are the result of accidental matings often end up in shelters. Once again they are taken from their mothers too young, usually at six weeks old, the earliest they can be weaned. Most puppies will never see their mothers or siblings again. In the wild dog families mainly stay together in packs. They may remain in these extended families for their entire lives. The puppies bred for human use, as companions, breeding bitches or working dogs will never experience this way of life. Effectively they have been sold and bought as slaves. Some people argue that humans and dog packs evolved together. Whilst ancient canines may have chosen to live alongside humans these days they have no choice in the matter. They are captives of the breeding industry. The stress for puppies starts inside the mothers then. Born to ailing bitches then sold as slaves to aliens.

Once in her human family a puppy can look forward to further stress. With her dog pack she would instinctively have learnt to communicate with body language, smell and scent marking. With humans she will have to learn to understand some language along with alien customs. In dog packs a lot of time is spent reassuring each other that all is well. In the hurly burly of a human family this need for reassurance may go unmet as it is unlikely to be a priority, or even in the awareness of the human pack.

A puppy will try to learn to adapt to her new environment but there will be gaps in the understanding between humans and the dogs. As much dog communication is body language humans wont understand or even notice, it is likely that much of the communication from a dog will be unseen or ignored. For a dog this must be like being sent to coventry forever.

To be a non human living in a human family is to be besieged by political dilemmas. The human family have all the power and control in the situation. In order to be allowed to walk, be fed and cared for a dog is obliged to comply to the will of all the humans. She may be given conflicting orders from family members, be subject to dangerous people or find herself in a dysfunctional family at risk of violence or abuse.

Where there is child abuse in a family or domestic violence what a burden this will place on a dog. Dogs read humans by the chemical smells we give off. They smell fear and unhappiness. At times when there is some sort of horror going on in a family the dog will smell, sense or hear it, often where it is missed by other family members. This will be another source of unrelenting stress on a dog.

Human expectation is another burden we ask our animal friends to carry. People may believe that by feeding, watering and walking our canine friends they are then obliged to love and obey us. They may agree, they may not. None the less we put them in situations virtually the whole time that are not of their choosing. We dictate the time of exercise, when they get to eat, where they go and who they see. This puts them in a state of perpetual infantalisation. Even when humans mean well they make assumptions about how dogs should behave in this unequal relationship with us. Again resulting in stress. In the wild, for example in a wolf pack, animal communities dictate their own rules. They exhibit complex, sustainable and sophisticated behaviors most of which is too subtle for humans to notice or understand. They are capable of feats of endurance and athleticism which could never be dreamt of, or equaled by humans. How must they feel being tied by a lead to a human of average intelligence, trundling round a park? So far so bad. Bred for money, kidnapped, dominated, misunderstood.

Then there is the built environment. The natural habitat of dog packs in the wild are various. Captive and domesticated animals are put into unnatural environments in our towns and cities that they do not understand. In the wild dogs will keep themselves safe from harm by understanding predator behavior. For example, travelling in a pack if there are predators around. In towns and cities hazards include traffic, as there are no visual or olfactory signals of danger with cars dogs may not view them as a hazard. To protect them from harm we tie them to us with leads, we tell them where they may go and how long they may go for. They are always dangling on a human arm.

Stress comes in many forms. One thing I made sure of with the dogs I cared for was that they were never left alone with children. This was for the protection of the dogs. There are gentle and thoughtful children around, there are also violent, uncaring and abusive young people. I decided never to subject my dogs to children at all. There are many reported incidents of where an adult has put children and dogs alone in situations where tragedy has occurred. Children may unwittingly transgress the boundries a dog may set on good behavior. For example touching food or toys belonging to the dog, or they may engage in cruel or aggressive behaviors that threaten or hurt the animal. If younger, the child may just flail about causing fear in the dog.

In my opinion a dog is never at fault for attacking a child because a human will always have put that dog in a vulnerable position either by letting the animal stray, leaving her alone with children, or abusing an animal in some way who then escapes attacking out of fear. In every instance, somewhere along the line, a human has put the dog in a dangerous situation. Dogs have no choice about the situations humans put them in, so they can bear no responsibility for an attack. A dog exhibiting aggression has been abused somewhere along the line, so in a situation where an attack has occurred there are two victims, the child and the dog. Once a child has been bitten by a dog the dog is then destroyed.

In human society not even men who rape and kill children get the death penalty. Murderers get bed and breakfast. There is no crime in the UK that humans can commit that results in them losing their lives , why then do we have a death penalty for dogs who have no control over what happens to them? This is a double standard and one that is clearly unfair to dogs. We need to locate responsibility with whoever allowed the situation to occur in the first place. This may not even be the carer of the dog. People open gates and let animals stray. They hit dogs and then leave them with children. They light incessant amounts of fireworks for weeks on end. We need public service announcements, common sense alerts. Do not hit, terrify or abuse your dog and never leave your dog alone with children. If we acted on this advice these tragedies would be avoided.

With all this in mind I never left any of my dogs alone with children. They were never subjected to the stress of being shouted at, teased or treated as a toy. People give animals to children to try to teach them responsibility. I feel Children need to be taught responsibility before they are allowed anywhere near a helpless and vulnerable creature.
Stress comes at dogs from every direction. People may engage in behaviors that stress dogs without even realising they are doing so. Next time you are around someone with a dog see if you can count the ways the animal is being subjected to stress. Has it got a lead or harness on? How is the lead being handled? Is the dog allowed to walk at her own pace and sniff or pee, or is she being hurried or dragged along by the neck. How would you feel if a bigger animal dragged you off to the toilet with a rope around your neck? If a dog is on an expanding lead does he get to go where he wants or does he have to stop at the extent of the lead just out of reach of interesting smells? Is the dog in a halti head collar? Is it fitted properly? I've often seen these on dogs heads pulled over the animals eyes. Head collars are not my idea of appropriate kit for dog walking. They are used to have more control over animals the carer deems needs to be more directed, perhaps with a dog someone thinks of as difficult. If you need to put one of these things on an animals head I would say the animal is unhappy with her situation. Happy dogs do not need onerous control. If you feel you need to restrain a dog at least buy her a comfortable harness and not drag her by the neck or head in uncomfortable kit.

One appalling method of controlling dogs that people use is the shock collar. When the collar is activated the dog gets an electric shock. The collar has a remote control. This, to my mind is abuse. I have seen one woman control a pack of six dogs with shock collars. The collars did not stop her dogs attacking a collie, they just hurt the dogs while they were doing it. I cannot ever see a situation that could justify a shock collar. Please never use one on a dog in your care.

Some dogs are taken for exercise by people on skateboards and bicycles. Often the dog is made to pull the person along, with the full weight of the human resting on the poor animals neck. This is dangerous, illegal in the UK and stressful for the dog.

Dogs need their own space, somewhere to retreat away from the family. Even dogs who love you may need time alone in safe space to relax. They may be feeling unsociable or ill or just tired from a walk. A dog will appreciate time on her own which will not be invaded by children or adults. The dogs I cared for had their own rooms to retreat to, to be away from each other when they needed to be. Dogs are pack animals and often love the families they are placed in but this does not have to mean constant contact.

Other dogs will thrive on company and get very stressed if left alone. They are individuals like humans, with varying experience of life. Give them a choice about how much human company they have. The dogs I cared for had their own rooms. If they chose they could socialise together, or retreat to be alone. Bramble and Sally would curl up alongside each other. Dreadlock and Floyd preferred their own company and would sleep out of sight of the others.

Noise can stress dogs. Border Collie Stan, Who lived in various places with Chris or I, didn't enjoy living in the town. He found the noisy drunks that passed his window terrifying and bustle in general caused his nerves to fray. Some breeds are ultra sensitive and will not thrive in a town.
Smells can cause stress and fear. Sometimes if someone in my terrace lit a bonfire the smell would pervade our house. The smoke that drifted in frightened Stan, who may have thought the house was on fire. He wouldn't have felt safe when his home smelt of smoke.

Constant bombardment with companionship may be okay for some dogs, for others the result is stress. A dog may not always want to be petted, fussed or pulled about by children.

Another stress for dogs is being left alone in cars. Many dogs each year die from overheating when carers lock them in vehicles. Even cars that are not overheating can be crashed into, or an animal may be teased or frightened through the glass. To a dog your car may feel like a mobile prison. They cannot get out on their own. My wish for dogs is that legislation will be brought in by governments to make it illegal to leave a dog alone in a car, in any circumstances, ever.

Excessive grooming, showing and traveling may stress animals, needless to say none of my companion animals were ever 'shown'. To my mind dog shows treat individual animals as meat to be prodded, poked and judged. Without being too crude how would you like to have your bottom prodded or testicles felt in an arena filled with strangers?

So far these things that stress dogs and ruin health have included the unwitting and thoughtless. There are also the times of huge trauma for animals such as the weeks every year when ear-splitting fireworks are let off. Barrage after barrage of high decibel terror are inflicted on wildlife and domestic animals. Rabbits cower in outside hutches and dogs freeze with fear in our homes. I've never understood why governments don't ban noisy fireworks. Silent ones are easily made. Someone somewhere is making lots of profit selling tranquilizing drugs to vets for dogs.

Dreadlock was one of those dogs that were terrified of fireworks. My solution was to put him in his van and drive up into the hills during the noisiest firework times. There we could watch the lights on the horizon without being plagued by loud noise. You cannot always escape from this though as the firework season is so long. This needs tougher legislation. Silent fireworks are the answer not medicating dogs.

I haven't touched on the deliberate cruelty and sadism to which some people subject dogs. What I want to convey is the huge role that stress plays in limiting dog longevity. If you use your imagination and try to put yourself in the position of a dog you should be able to avoid at least some of these situations. You can then begin to build relaxation into the life of the dog in your care.

Think what your dog enjoys, if it's long walks, do them. If it's ball games, play them. If it's the company of other dogs, find them. If it's peace and quiet, enable it. Most dogs prefer being outdoors to in. Facilitate it. At times you will have to be out and leave a dog at home. Walk with her well beforehand. Maybe feed her, if it's time, then with her physical needs catered for she may just fall asleep. Never leave her alone for too long. Too long will mean different things to different animals, various dog organisations will say four hours is the absolute maximum you should ever leave a dog alone. For an animal that has seperation anxiety that would be way too long. My feeling is if you work full time and there is no one on hand to care for the dog while you are out, don't have one.

As dogs experience cycles of time differently than humans, four hours alone may seem like twenty eight to a dog. If they can't even get into the garden to pee while your gone this is way too long.

It makes sense when looking for a dog to care for, to find an individual of a breed or cross breed that may have characteristics that compliment your own and fit in with the way you live your life.

Breeds that are currently fashionable like huskys are beautiful and amazing creatures, but unless you like fifteen mile walks every day and can cater to specialist needs they are better left to those with boundless energy and specialist knowledge. Crossbred dogs are said to maintain better health than pedigrees with less inherited health problems. They are said to have hybrid vigor. Bramble and Floyd, who were the oldest of the dogs in my care, were rarely ill. Floyd was a springer spaniel and border collie cross and Bramble was border collie who may have had another breed in the mix. Dreadlock was a German shepherd and lived to fifteen, which is good for that breed. He was carefully managed to age. The breed of dog you choose to acquire will have an impact on the animals longevity.

Some of the larger breeds do not live long. Some will not even make ten years old. If you are looking for longevity I believe medium sized dogs fare best. You can still maximise their longevity with the right care but you know from the outset that say, a Newfoundland with heart problems will die sooner than a medium sized or smaller dog. All dogs deserve our care. Decide how much time you are realistically prepared to spend walking with a dog. Think about whether you are prepared to do a lot of grooming and if not don't acquire someone with lots of long hair. Think of how much you want to spend on food and vets fees. Read as much as you can about different breeds and then speak to rescue centres and tell them what you can offer a dog. If you cannot commit to a regular routine of feeding, grooming, walking and some vets visits please get a cuddly toy instead of an animal. Having spent my entire adult life looking after dogs I would say never underestimate the amount of work that caring for them entails.

Consider what age dog you can cope with. If you haven't cared for one before I would steer clear of puppies. Stating the obvious, a puppy is a baby dog. They need as much care as a human baby. You will have taken her from her mother when she has just been weaned. She will be dependant on you for everything. Foods, liquids, cleaning up urine and faeces until she is housetrained. People do leave puppies alone, but I believe that is entirely inappropriate. This is a helpless animal child looking to you for everything she needs for protection and care. If you cannot provide for a demanding baby, get an older dog. Human babies need feeding, potty training, keeping clean, lots of company. There is much similarity with looking after very young dogs. Just as you would never leave a human baby alone for hours, unless you were criminally negligent, you should never do this with the baby of a dog. You may want to consider what you can offer an animal. A base line should be adequate income to feed one. Time, energy, patience and willingness to provide appropriate care. Those people who buy dogs as accessories or as toys for children are not the places which make the best homes for dogs.

An important consideration for new dog carers is where to find a dog. Personally I have never bought a dog from a breeder. To me this would feel like I was buying a slave. Just as humans cannot buy children. I do not believe dogs should be bred to make money. Rescue shelters kill many healthy dogs each year because they cannot afford to keep them alive. I would like to see all breeding made illegal and legislation passed so only shelter dogs were offered up for homing. What is the point of allowing individuals to make money producing more dogs while so many unfortunate creatures are killed or kept in shelters for months and even years at a time? People say some shelter dogs may have unpredictable temprements. That is entirely true, but if you cannot cope with that possibility you are better off with a robot or virtual pet.

All animals are individuals with idiosyncrasies, peccadilloes, learned or instinctive behaviors. They will have likes and dislikes. They will have opinions. Do not expect compliance or an unproblematic time, you are taking on a living being with her own inner landscape. It is my firm belief that she will be as intelligent as you, and be of equal worth. Don't think of her as an acquisition or purchase. Think of taking her on as adopting a family member. Get your attitude right before you start out.

Coming into your home from a shelter, or anywhere else will be a complete change for the dog, a break from a routine she was used to. She may be recovering from illness, ill treatment, abuse or homelessness as a stray. Make the transition to your home as easy as possible for her. Make sure she has a dedicated space of her own, a comfortable bed, water on hand always, appropriate, adequate food, leave her some biscuits around and get her into a gentle routine of exercise, company and care.

Please understand the obvious, You are dealing with another species of animal, she may not understand what you expect from her, or anything you say. If you take on an older dog familiar with human language she may understand most of what you say, you cannot make assumptions initially. Care should be calm, quiet and non intrusive, building trust as you go along. This is done by providing for all her needs for food, exercise and companionship and by being kind and non confrontational. Do not take offence if your wishes are misunderstood or not followed. You have essentially taken on an individual who didn't ask to come into your life. Treat her as a respected friend and deal with any issues carefully as they arise.

Animals that present challenges may have been abused, exploited or beaten. Never meet challenges with violence or anger. Emotion should be kept out of untangling these difficulties. When Dreadlock was around I sometimes felt that he was a little over assertive with Chris. At the time I was on a course learning about neurolinguistic programming so I could incorporate it into my counselling practice. I asked my educator, who also kept large dogs, how he handled this sort of issue. He told me a story. He used to be an advocate and befriender of young men on probation, some of whom had been involved in violence. He knew a particular lad who used to hit a dog in his care. The young man had been brought up by a violent father who hit him. When trying to change the behavior of the dog the lad would hit him to try and get him to behave. He asked my educator about better ways of changing the dogs behavior. My educator said as an example, imagine you have a dog who keeps peeing on your flower beds, The simplest way to change this is to put up a fence in front of the flowers. The dog will then avoid them. Undesirable behavior then stops. The young man said he would have hit the dog. The trainer said if you put up a fence there will be no point in the transaction between you and the animal where hitting him would have helped at all. The dog will just become fearful and resentful. The point he was trying to instill in the boy is you can go round things and avoid confrontation. There is never a situation where hitting an animal helps. This is abuse and has no place in dog care.

Any behavior from a new dog that causes problems, such as peeing in an undesirable place, needs to be achieved with intelligence not violence. If you think along those lines much can be resolved. Essentially a dog is her own person, you can hope she will fit in with your life, family or expectations but you have no right to demand. A dog that has serious issues or that you feel is beyond your ability to cope with is better off with someone who may better understand her needs. Choosing a companion carefully, maybe visiting a few times and going out for walks, will save heartache and stress for all later on.

Anyone wanting to provide a dog with the best possible environment would do well to learn about vegan, animal rights philosophy. A vegan is someone who lives on a plant based diet and refuses to eat meat, fish or dairy products. Vegans don't wear leather, wool, silk or feathers. They avoid using products tested on animals and promote animal rights. If you want a dog in your care to live a long life vegan philosophy will provide you with lots of tools and ideas to help.

The reason vegans don't use any animal products is so as not to contribute to animal suffering. Animals used for food, for example cows, pigs and chickens, live miserable lives full of pain and fear. They are trapped in abusive systems such as factory farms. They live frightened and painful lives, often in dirty, overcrowded factory systems. They are sent to slaughterhouses where they meet their deaths in terror and many die in terrible pain. Stunning animals doesn't always work, and some animals such as baby chicks are put through grinders to be killed while alive and conscious. We cannot even imagine the agony they suffer. At best a cow may have a bolt shot through her head before she is dismembered. At worst an animal watches others die, and dies herself screaming in pain.

Cows used for dairy production suffer terribly. In order to produce milk, a cow must be kept lactating by being made repeatedly pregnant. Her calves will be taken from her at birth so humans can use the milk. The female calf may be kept to repeat the cycle of exploitation to produce more dairy. The male calf who is of no use to the farmer will be immediately shot. Many calves are sent abroad to be kept in veal crates, deprived of a proper diet. They live short lives filled with suffering and pain. Cows are made pregnant mostly by artificial insemination, with a contraption called a rape rack.

Fish for human consumption die painful deaths drowned in air. For these reasons vegans refuse to eat or wear animal products There are also health implications with the consumption of animal products. One recent study concluded that vegans live thirteen years longer than meat eaters or vegetarians. Factory farmed animals are also filled with antibiotics and other medications. This has implications for human health and disease resistance as animal products are tainted by drugs.

Vegans believe that all animals, both human and non human, should be able to exist without exploitation. They believe animals deserve lives free from pain and suffering. Vegans do not believe that some animals are more important than others. They do not see the sense in killing a cow to feed a dog. If you can learn about veganism and animal rights philosophy you have the possibility of transforming how you think of animals and how you decide to treat them. If you want a dog to have a long life you can embrace a vegan and animal rights philosophy. You are then in a position to better understand their management and care. Along with appropriate food, exercise and stress control becoming vegan and understanding animal rights philosophy is the best advice I can offer someone who wants to promote the conditions to enable long life in a dog.

Environment counts. Like humans, animals need space to exercise, thrive and play. Dogs will find more interest in natural, outdoor environments than in a built up city or town. So much of our countryside is now under pressure from developers obsessed with profit. Places to walk with a dog become less every day. Urban sprawl eats into the buffer zones and spreads like a cancer into the countryside. Precious green space is built on. Traffic and human activity despoil what environment we have left. If you want there to always be somewhere rural to walk your dog and enjoy watching the wildlife I recommend you campaign to save green spaces.

Vitally also, your own sense of self will impact on how you are able to look after others, canine or human. People who are confident and secure in their own identity, happy in their skin, will make the best carers. Those with insecurities or something to prove may be too intent on controlling others, be they dogs or people, to enable those in their care to flourish. It goes without saying that no one with too many personal issues should take on the management of vulnerable animals.

These then are some of the secrets of managing a dog for longevity. Get her food right, give her lots of exercise, watch her stress levels are kept down and get your attitude right. If there was just one thing I could instill in you to remember in your dog care it would be to develop what I think of as a vegan attitude. Respect the dog in your care and treat her like the individual she is. Think of her as an equal family member, and not just the pet on the floor. If you can manage most of this you have a fighting chance of enabling her to reach her natural potential and live as long as possible.

Brambles fields disappear under concrete

Chapter Eight.

Caring for elderly creatures.

Dreadlock was still eating well, enjoying time outside and according to the vet, not in any pain. With Chris on hand to help manage him he was enjoying his old age. My father was getting on a bit by then also. He had been knocked off his pushbike by a motorbike years before and this had left him with pins in his leg and a bend from knee to foot, which curtailed his mobility to a degree. As he had never learned to drive he still cycled about albeit slowly, scooting along the pavement. At eighty one he still liked to get into the town most days to shop and meet his friends for lunch. One of his favourite haunts was a restaurant near Bridgwaters Cornhill. He would make his way slowly into town, lock his bike to a drainpipe and amble into lunch to meet his friends carrying his old black canvas shopping bag.

Joining them for a meal I got to hear what all the pensioners were talking about. My aunt, mums sister, was coming up to retirement age and worrying about managing on a small pension. Dads friend Molly, a widow living alone had fallen downstairs, and later tripped up on the pavement. The talk at lunch was all about the difficulty of pensioners living on tiny incomes despite having been employed all their lives and then how they all managed their various aches and pains. Dad was on medication for his heart and warfarin to thin his blood. He had booked himself in for a flu jab and was on painkillers to try to stop the fierce ache that never let up, in his knee. My own problems with mobility continued going into winter and we all huddled around steaming drinks, a small enclave of mutual support grumbling in turn about our various difficulties.

In the afternoon I planned to drive my van with Dreadlock up to Wind down and let him enjoy the fresh air for a couple of hours. My mind drifted off to things I had to do that day, while I listened to the companionable chatter of dad and his friends. Molly, it seemed had been to the cake shop, tasked by dad to buy him an enormous latticed pastry roll. Molly had bought herself a bit of takeaway and mums sister had a cake. Instead of ordering lunch in the restaurant that day the pensioners had brought their own. "Dad" I said, mortified that we would be thrown out on our ears "You can't buy food elsewhere and bring it in here to eat, we'll be thrown out". Dads response was to send Molly up to the cutlery trolley to fetch condiments and napkins with which to eat their booty in the corner of the room.
The anarchist pensioners ate their fill and drunk their health right under the watchful eye of the restaurants c.c.t.v. Dad hid his pastry roll on his lap and stopped chewing each time the waitress passed, managing to give her a smile with his mouth clamped firmly shut. Molly ate her potato and my aunt brushed sugar crumbs off her chin. "We've got away with it" dad said sensing victory. Just as they were congratulating themselves on their audacity at having contrived to eat their lunch in the warm for nothing, the waitress passed."Can I get you people something?" she asked "or have you had enough already" Brushing past the table her eyes rested briefly on the condiments and napkins and she gave a slight cough.

I left the band of elderly brigands discussing what they would do to the blasted government if they got their hands on them and drove home to pick up Dreadlock. It was a cold day so Chris loaded lots of blankets into the van and made a comfy rest for the old dog so he would keep warm on the drive. The van laboured up the steep hill climbing round the winding lanes. As the drivers seat is high up I could see all over the hedges, there was a clear blue sky with a few white clouds floating above the fields, some of which had been ploughed or had the remainder of stubbly plants left in from earlier crops of oil rape seed.

At Wind Down Chris gently helped Dreadlock out of the back of the van. As he alighted our Robin friend appeared calling to us, possibly asking for food. Chris left Dreadlock with me and climbed back into the van to fetch his trolley which he helped the elderly dog onto so he could pull him round the forest circuit. These were the last precious days of Dreadlock and unbeknownst to me then, my fathers life. Both the old chaps needed a hand here and there now to maintain their lifestyles and for both of them it was to be their last few months alive. Dreadlock enjoyed the slow trundle around Wind Down, sitting up on his trolley with his blanket covering his thick yellow and black fur. On the downhill slopes he banged his paw on the trolley which I thought translated to "faster please dad". There were few people about and the ones we saw we knew. One elderly chap laughed at the spectacle of Chris pulling the big Alsatian on the trolley. "Shouldn't that be the other way round?" he said "Not if you're a Vegan" Chris muttered into his jumper. We stayed at Wind Down playing catch the fir cone and shake the banana skin with Dreadlock until it was time to leave. The winter sun made a beautiful picture of burning orange filtered through the conifer trees. Deer began their evening amble across the forest and the Robin left us to go back to rest in a tree. We drove slowly back down the hill with the sunset behind us all the way home. At the other end Chris unloaded Dreadlock and took him into the house, he then returned to the van to unload the trolley and gather up Dreadlock's bowl and water bottles. Then was time to change his water and feed him before he settled down to sleep.

Sometimes Dreadlock would feed himself and other times he asked for help by lying next to his food and looking up to Chris. I think in his old age, after a busy afternoon he was just too tired to stand, so Chris fed him by hand and then tucked him into his bed.
This was the daily routine on days when my back was up to it, other times Chris had to manage Dreadlock on his own. I would go along carrying a stick, bent over like an old lady and at these times Dreadlocks eyes were full of fellow feeling. Two ageing creatures together.

As the months slipped into the next year I began to worry about dad. He would sometimes turn up for lunch in a jumper stained with food, I wasn't sure if he hadn't seen it due to poor eyesight or if he was having trouble washing his clothes. Molly was helping him out a lot despite being in her mid eighties herself. She would fetch his prescriptions from the chemist, buy clothes or food for him and in return he would buy lunch for her and her family. Sometimes mum would appear if we could entice her from her cozy flat and occasionally my sister would visit from the coast and take photos. My elderly parents began to remind me of big old bears, slow, gentle and thoughtful. Photos taken at the time have so much poignancy for the now; the last year my parents ate together. In the November of that year dad got ill. He was continuing on the Warfarin and then he had a flu jab. I read later this combination can cause serious problems. On the Saturday night I called to visit dad and shouted hello as I entered the hallway. Usually there would be an answering shout back, this evening there was nothing. "Dad?" I shouted again, feeling slightly peeved at being ignored.

The light in the front sitting room was on and I could see it under the crack of the door. I didn't understand why he wasn't answering. Slowly I turned the brass door knob on the cream paneled door and it opened into the room. The television was on quietly, which was quite unusual as dad was quite deaf and for a minute I wondered if he had been murdered, or if someone had broken into the house. Quickly scanning the room and in the dazzle of light the figure of dad, very still and slumped in his old leather chair, became apparent. He had blood congealed on his head and his face was very red "Dad what's happened?" I asked him. Looking up very slowly dad tried to articulate his words, "Fell downstairs yesterday" he told me softly "Fell backwards off the fourth stair". He was looking at me in puzzlement as if memory was an effort " I couldn't get up, I fell into the recycling bin and got stuck there...I was on the floor for eleven hours. I've just been sat here since, couldn't seem to move much." I turned back into the hallway and dialed for an ambulance. While we were waiting dad filled me in a little more, it seems he had gone to his G.P. the day before and had his flu jab but didn't feel right after it and on going up to bed had taken the dreadful tumble.

The doctors arrived quickly and examined dad in his chair, one said he thought he should go to hospital. Dad declined. The other doctor said he might be okay to stay in his chair. The paramedics called and put dad back upstairs in his bed, he was very dehydrated so they put a line in him and dripped in some water. Dad lay in the bed looking frail and terribly old, "It's so cold with the water going in" he said, although after he was rehydrated he looked a little livelier. He lay in bed and tried to talk to me. "I was naked in the hallway" he said "If the heating hadn't been on I would have frozen to death". After handing him a bottle to wee in I was about to leave the room. "Anne" he said, calling me back "could you put the blankets over my face so I can sleep?" As I began to pull the thick cream blankets up around his neck he looked into my eyes and said " Thank you for what you've done for me." I felt like dad was saying goodbye and I wanted to thank him back. "Thanks for looking after me when I was young". I told him "You've worked hard all your life and kept a roof over our heads and fed us. Thanks dad, I love you m'dear." Dad closed his eyes and sighed. "Turn the light out will you?" He said as I left the room.

I decided to make phone calls. My siblings would have to be told dad had had a fall. I phoned my sister in Bournemouth and told her that dad had probably had a stroke and that she should come home. She said that she would phone work and tell them that she had an emergency and then she would jump on a train. I asked her to call my brother and to tell him what had happened, although eventually it transpired my brother had already called before dad had fallen down.

One of the doctors had said dad should go to hospital to ascertain if he'd definitely had a stroke. I set about trying to persuade him. He said he was worried about catching M.R.S.A. and wouldn't be leaving his home. Trying to work out what to do for the best I rang an acquaintance who works in the social services and asked her how I ought to proceed. As dad was refusing hospital she advised me to try to get funding for carers to come into dad's home. After some phone calls and an assessment the local authority agreed to provide carers and nurses twice a day. So four lots of people who he didn't know would be calling on the old chap. "I don't want all these people in and out" he said. I pointed out that the family couldn't manage him on our own.

During the next fortnight the family pleaded with dad to try to get him to go into hospital. We all felt ill equipped to care for a seriously ill, elderly man. The nurses were wonderful, headed up by a brisk, no nonsense lady called Rowena who was firm but gentle with dad. They developed some minor banter, as much as you can with a very sick man who is fading and withdrawing before your eyes. "It's me, Rowena" she would say when she came in and dad would reply "Oh no, not you". It had become apparent to me that dad was slowly dying. Despite our constant care and love for him he had begun to drift away from us. He had initially had some dialogue when we tried to persuade him to go to hospital but after telling us to shut up and that he was going to stay home, his communication became less and less. He would still ask us to pass him his bottle to urinate into, but other than that he began to stop speaking. We knew he could speak if he wanted to because when his doctor arrived he thanked the man for his care over the years, but increasingly if we asked him anything there was no reply. It was as if having said his thanks to me he had nothing more to say.

Here and there we had continued to beg him to go to hospital but still he refused point blank. The ambulance service and nurses had told us that if he was mentally competent we couldn't override his wishes and oblige him to go into hospital care. It was as if he had made up his mind to die. I think with his constant knee pain and now leg ulcers, he was plagued with anxiety and no doubt the stroke had affected his outlook. The family was under great strain because we didn't want to lose him but the constant caring was producing huge stress. I was spending much of the time with dad. My sister who had come home from Bournemouth was doing the night shifts with dad, due to my back problems there was no way I could stay up all night. My brother did a couple of nights on call with the old man but said his girlfriend didn't want him to do anymore. Eventually seventy six year old mum got roped in, and although by then they had been living separately for over a decade she got stuck in and sat up all night with dad on a hard and unforgiving chair. She said he seemed comfortable but I don't think they talked much. One thing he said to her was "Have you come to get your housekeeping?" and mum replied "No Roy, I've come to look after you." The two old companions spent dads last days quietly together in the downstairs front room that had been adapted with an electronic hospital bed. It had an air mattress that constantly moved slightly so that the patient wouldn't get pressure sores and this made spooky little noises and creakings all through the night.

Chris was at Wellington road managing Puck, a new dog we had taken on when tasked with finding him a home by an ex employer of his. The employer had temporarily split with his wife who was moving out of her house. She was going to move into rented accommodation where she couldn't take a dog. Despite much ringing around no dogs home had space to take the soon to be homeless animal. The woman he lived with told us he was twelve years old although he looked much younger. After having no success at finding Puck a home the carer said she would have to put him to sleep. By then Chris had taken him for one or two walks due to his carer having a degree of agrophobia. Neither Chris nor I could bear to see this shiny, energetic dog put to death with a needle due to circumstances beyond his control and when there was nothing physically wrong with him. We took him on although I wasn't sure about the wisdom of it because Dreadlock was frail by then and might feel his replacement had been brought into the house. Nonetheless Puck was about to be put to sleep so we took him in and kept him separate from Dreadlock with his bed in the downstairs front room. As with the Collies exercise Chris walked with Puck and Dreadlock separately, that way Puck got to hare around at speed and Dreadlock could amble at his own pace. By the time dad got ill Dreadlock had died so it was only Puck at home to care for.

Life at dads house was becoming increasingly stressful. The actual caring was fairly straight forward, the main thing was to keep dad as hydrated as possible because his kidneys, problematic before, were getting worse. We had to keep offering him measured amounts of water to sip and then he wanted a wee, this too had to be measured. Dad had stopped eating entirely after a while and then even the little bits of ice cream he had been accepting before were being left on the spoon. As a family we had started to bicker. I felt some people weren't pulling their weight and my sister wasn't coping well with the nights. Mutually supportive at the outset the family began to fracture and upsetting arguments began to ensue. We tried to keep our problems away from the dying man but every so often someone would have a last gasp attempt to persuade him into hospital.

Nerves had begun to fray, near the end of his life dads kidneys were failing and even being touched gently began to hurt him. When the carers changed his sheets he had to stay in bed and be rolled onto his side to pull the sheets from under him, although they did their best dad would scream and cry out piteously in pain as they moved him. I asked Rowena if they could stop moving him to wash him because he began to express fear when the carers came near, expecting every light touch to hurt him. Rowena said he couldn't be left in a mess, even though it hurt him to be moved. I had been standing by the bed to talk to dad while the carers washed him to try to distract him from the pain, but his pitiful screams as they moved him to change the bed or wash him began to really upset me and so when the carers came I had taken to standing in the kitchen with my fingers in my ears trying to avoid hearing dads agonised cries.

Going home to spend time with puck I couldn't help noticing the difference in the vigor of this healthy, bouncing animal and my poor, dear old dad. Puck was almost as old as dad in dog years, his twelve years corresponding to him being about seventy four in human years to dads eighty two. Where dad had eaten lots of rubbish near the end of his life and had the odd drink to assuage the pain of his knee, Puck was being fed measured amounts of food. Where dad had started to downgrade his exercise and eat lunch in the town rather than walk, Puck was out and about at all hours tramping the river pathway with Chris. Now dad was dying in his bed while Puck bounced like a two year old out into the street.

Dad was in a lot of pain in his later years and after his accident. He took lots of prescription medication relying on doctors to manage his health. Where, when slightly younger he had eaten lots of fruit and veg and cycled around, as he aged he began to want to cook less and his exercise became limited. The medication he was on put a strain on his kidneys and he began to drink a little more at night. Inch by inch dad was digging his grave by lessening his exercise and eating the wrong food. Maybe he compensated for the loneliness he said he felt in his old age, despite family visiting I think he missed the company of the workers, mainly men who in his capacity as union secretary, he had represented all of his working life. Certainly he still enjoyed the occasional trips he made for meals and meetings with the retired members section of the union. As well as his failing health I think he sort of died from a broken heart; Maybe he felt his useful and comradely days were over and in his latter years the times he could get out for lunch with friends was the most interesting company he got.

Dads time was drawing near. His weight over the two weeks of confinement to bed had dropped markedly. Always a *bon viver* dad had been portly, now he had shrunk. His face once round and red changed shape drastically and without his teeth in I hardly recognised him as my father. Mum said he had begun to look more like the Rawles side of the family now his face was thinner. One day when I reached dads house I began to feel very uneasy. Some instinct told me something was changing. I became convinced that he needed to go into hospital there and then or he would die. In retrospect that may have been when septicemia set in and my unconscious mind picked up on some sort of chemical changes. I felt depressed and helpless that dad would not go into hospital to try at least to recover. I went to the front bedroom and sat in the light from the window ruminating on all my troubles. All dad had to do was stop being stubborn, I decided. He needed to go into hospital, be put on an intravenous drip, which wasn't possible at home and with professional care and rehabilitation he would get over the stroke.

I flew downstairs full of indignation and went into his room. "Dad you've got to go to hospital, I don't want you to die". Dad said nothing and I noticed one of his eyes was wide open while the other had started to close. Defeated I drove home and lay in a bath trying to stop thinking, at least for an hour. That night on one of my brothers two night shifts with dad, the old man who had worked so hard for the men in his union, and who had cared for me for my entire life, passed away. My brother said he had gone upstairs to lie down when he became aware of a noise and when he went down to check on dad the old chap had stopped breathing. When I got there in the morning he had been dead for a while. Dad died on a cold winter night, shortly before my fiftieth birthday.

He had made eighty two years old, Bramble made twenty five. In human terms that is one hundred and seventy five years old. With humans it is harder to try to keep people alive. People sabotage their health inadvertently. They mostly know what they should eat and that they should take exercise. Things like loneliness can lead to compensating with food or booze. With dogs you can guard against this problem, whereas human emotion can lead to self destruction this does not happen to dogs. As you are your dogs carer you can make sure she eats well, you can promote and monitor exercise, you can enable positive health and keep her company. The saying is true, use it or lose it. While dad at the end was taking little exercise Bramble was doing the same amount as ever right up until she died. Apart from the brief time around her accident she continued to have the same amount of time as she always had outdoors. It was a little slower as she aged and we adjusted our pace to hers and when she was injured we took her swimming, when Dreadlock became ill we lavished him with care. Dads life had gone out of control I think. His loneliness had caused him to turn to junk food after years of eating healthily. After his accident his mobility became less and constant pain stopped him wanting to move. Bramble was kept to a regular routine of walks four times a day and constant care. She was given the same amount of attention my family gave to my dying father. An old creature, human and non human, is a similar prospect to manage. For manage and orchestrate you must to promote the longest lives. Longevity in all creatures be they dogs or fathers, must be designed and crafted. If you want dogs in your care to flourish and thrive for longer this is what it takes; information, hard work, attention to detail and ongoing, infinite care.

Dad retires from the post office engineering union

Nos da Bramble

Chapter Nine.

Bramble Dies

Bramble, Sally and Stan were laid out on their divan bed. The bitches lay close together and Stan stretched out at a respectful distance a few feet away.

While I brushed Bramble I liked to tell the dogs stories about things Bramble had done in her youth. Stan would fall asleep listening to the soft drone of my voice and Sally would kiss my face. Bramble basked in the attention of hearing her name mentioned in the same sentence as the words fierce, park walks and chasing. As she got older Sally had taken her place at the head of the pack so I liked to make a fuss of Bramble and remind her of her halcyon days.

This evening I was talking to Bramble about the time when she, Floyd and I were walking in the Hamp fields. Bramble and Floyd started barking and when I got to where they were stood I could see they had cornered a young fox by the stream. Floyd was on one side of the terrified creature and Bramble the other. They looked at me clearly thinking that they had caught our supper and were waiting for me to kill the fox and drag her home. They were more surprised when I shouted at them to leave her alone and gave them a lecture about not stalking the wildlife. They looked at each other in great puzzlement. Bramble who had listened to the fox tale before always looked pleased when I told her she was kind to let the creature go. The gentle brushing and the familiar story worked their magic and soon all the dogs were snoring quietly on their bed.

Once they were asleep I leant back into the wall at the side of the bed and began to feel tired myself. My mind drifted back to the events that had happened over the many years I had known Bramble. So many memories. Life had been a real struggle early on.

Financially there had been very tough times. Neither Chris nor I had ever had a job that paid over the minimum wage, and even as house sharers we hardly earned enough to pay our halves of the bills. At one point we had been unable to pay an electricity bill and the power company turned our supply off. We had to cook on a picnic stove using little gas cylinders, heat the house with calor gas which smelt, and use candles for light.

Two memories flashed through my mind in quick succession, one was the night I was trying to plan the next springs food planting by reading a seed catalogue in my bedroom with a candle. I had been writing down the reference numbers of broad beans and carrot names when my candle burnt out and the room plunged into darkness. It was a very bleak time in the small house in Ashleigh terrace. I began to despair. How would I feed a dog with no supplement of home grown veg from the garden? I made my way downstairs to the back room which looked out on the back of the house. A full moon had illuminated the scene and I could see a cat sat on the shed roof watching for wildlife in the moonlight. I sat on the settee next to Floyd who leaned against me in companionable silence. Tears of exasperation began to trickle down my face. Everything was so hard and I didn't know how we would make it through. Floyd was never one to show emotion, being a clever and practical creature. What she did was to get up and start pushing at the back of the sofa with her nose. I couldn't work out what she was doing then I noticed she was putting her nose on the big printed flowers on the textile that covered the furniture. She as trying to move the roses

92

around. This struck me as very funny and my self pity and anxiety turned to guffaws of laughter. Floyd put a premtory paw on my arm. As with so many times in my life Floyd saved me from myself. It was hard to wallow in self pity with such an amusing and positive creature around.

Instead of waiting for penury to come and get me I decided I would have to sell some furniture in the morning. I had a big velvet armchair with posh braids of velvet on the arms. It was an antique I had brought from a junk shop. If I could sell it to an antique dealer it should make a couple of quid. Then there was an oak table I'd brought from a friend which opened up to expand and was the sort of thing quite sought after in the middle class terraces at the edge of where I lived. In the morning I rung a dealer I knew of and she sent a man round to pick up the big chair, the oak table and some heavy velvet curtains with an art deco motif that I thought might make a few more pounds. The guy handed me over a couple of notes and I watched as his van drove off taking the only nice things we had in the house.

As he left the postman came up the path and I felt a flash of fear churn my stomach. Two brown and one white envelope lay in the hallway between two doors. Bills we couldn't pay! I stood by the front room door for a minute paralyzed by fear. I thought I might be going to have an asthma attack from the stress of poverty. As I stood by the door willing myself to pick up the bills two large men marched up the path of our small terrace and hammered on the door. I couldn't imagine who they were, but they seemed to mean business with what was almost a policeman's knock. My natural instinct was to remain by the front room door as still as a rabbit who has been spotted by a fox. The men banged on the door again and the ghastly knock echoed like thunder in the hallway. One of the men said to the other "I suppose they were expecting the bailiffs to call". He snorted with laughter while his friend sniggered "I can see there's no furniture in the front room. They've even removed the curtains. I think they've moved out". His mate joined him in regarding the empty downstairs room through the window. Then they turned down the path to go. "Almost glad they weren't in" said the tallest man "Last time I called the woman who lives here swore at me like a trooper."

Relief flooded through me like a river that has been undammed. The Autumn day was bright and cool, I decided that I would visit my friend Pearl in her nice middle class home on the other side of town. She would be cheering optimistic company and there would be herbal tea and most important of all electric light. I was sick of trying to read seed catalogues in the light of a candle, or having to wait for moonlight before I could see to cut my toenails. I went into town on my secondhand but lovely bike. It was an old gents model, the sort that elderly men parked next to their allotments. I'd tarted it up with streamers on the handlebars, a bag on the back and a big bell. Then I'd painted it red, orange and yellow with old tins of paint I'd found under the stairs. I cycled down to the health food shop and bought big bags of brown rice and red split lentils. I picked up the mock beef textured vegetable protein that the dogs ate and a bar of vegan chocolate for myself. Balancing it on the crossbar of the bike I rode home the pretty way past hedges filled with hawthorn berries along the grey lane that was on the edge of our estate. It was blackberry time and the lane was full of them. I stopped the bike and picked as many as I could carry in my bag on the way home.

Floyd was stretched out by the back door when I got in and I let her out into the garden where she had a pee before she ambled back into her room. Chris came through the front door just as I was about to walk with the dogs and said "I'll take them to the fields while you visit Pearl". I cycled the fifteen minute journey to the other side of town where my parents, who weren't speaking to me at the time, lived. My mother had thrown a hissy fit when I said I was gay and my father said I should stop visiting causing trouble by upsetting my mum. Pearl who was thirty years older than me was a sort of mum substitute or at least a maternal influence when I wasn't visiting my parents home. I knocked on the door in anticipation of a warm welcome, a cup of tea and the bright lights of someone's sitting room. Pearl opened the door and was pleased to see me. She ushered me into her front parlor and asked me if I wanted tea. Just as I was beginning to feel maybe life would work out after all Pearl turned the light off and lit a candle. "I thought we could have an evening by candlelight" she said, " So much more relaxing don't you think?" She couldn't quite work out what she'd said wrong when her guest turned pale with horror and began making excuses to leave.

As I rode home it started to rain. The autumn air was tinged with cold. At Ashleigh terrace the calor gas was running out and I'd spent the furniture money on food. There was nothing left to buy gas with. Tomorrow I would have to put something to sell in the local auction. I didn't have much left. The thing that was painted like a rainbow would have to be sold. My bike would have to go. Returning home I pushed the wet machine through the front door where water dripped off it and made small puddles in the hall. Floyd looked up from her seat on the sofa and regarded me with a questioning look. She got up to stretch, then came over to me wagging her tail. "It's getting worse" I told her. "I don't know how we're going to manage".

The next day I washed and spruced up my bicycle and rode it for the last time down to the market place in Bridgwater where the weekly auction took place. It was quite a colourful affair. Two elderly women ran it and although we already had the decimal system of coinage they liked to calculate their profits in the old system of pounds, shillings and pence. This made bidding quite a challenge for some of the younger people who had never had to deal with that way of adding. The hall was crowded as usual. It had long trestle tables of second hand goods all around the side. They were marked with lot numbers. There were a few cycles, the odd chair, an aluminium ladder, boxes of the tat of desperate people, eggs, veg and flowers and now my beautiful rainbow bike. One of the auctioneers, Miss Ashe gave me a number to put on my bike for the auction. Number 27. It was the last of my chattels to go. Now I would have no worldly goods.

The auction started with Miss Ashe holding up various pieces of kit that no one much wanted, or some things that everyone did which would push up the bid. Finally the auction moved onto number 27. My bike. "What am I bid for this colourful contraption?" Miss Ashe asked the tightly packed crowd. I felt sad it was going, but also a shiver of anticipation. Maybe I would get as much as ten pounds. That would feed the dogs for ages. No one said anything for a minute, and everything was still, save a curl of foul smoke drifting up to the ceiling from one old chaps cigar. Eventually someone said "I'll bid two pounds". My eyes bulged with annoyance. Two pounds! I'd rather starve to death, I thought to myself. Eventually after a bit of banter an elderly middle class man bought it for his grandson. My bike was going to live at the posh end of town. He paid seven pounds for my kaleidoscope of colour and I picked the money up at the auctions end from Miss Ashe who took some of it for herself to pay towards her wages and the rent of the hall. It took a while to walk home that day, sans bicycle, but when I got there the dogs were curled up under the window asleep with their long eyelashes resting on beautiful faces and I felt relief. At least I could feed them for a few more days.

The time at Ashleigh terrace was very hard, but it was the first real home I'd had after leaving my parents. I'd grown lots of veg there and created a beautiful, if modest garden. Many times later on after Floyd had died I longed to be able to go back into the past for just a day to those hard times where at least I had my beautiful Collie friends with me. Always loving and accepting of whatever the day would bring. Bramble was still snoring next to sally on the bed and Sam was farting in his sleep. It was warm and unusually quiet in the front room at Wellington road as I sat and remembered where I'd come from. In an hour or two the pubs would be throwing out their army of drunken customers. Many of whom would be filing past my house. From about eleven thirty to four a.m. it would be too noisy and alarming to sleep as mainly men staggered down our road throwing glass bottles to the floor and pulling wing mirrors off our cars.

Stan and Dreadlock hated weekends in Bridgwater. Dreadlock would refuse to take a late night walk and Stan would go out for a pee with his head down, looking wary and hurry back in. Bramble was a little deaf by the time we had moved to Wellington road so she missed a lot of the noise and slept soundly, and Sally didn't care. If anyone had threatened her whilst walking she would have thrown herself at them with a sneer and got stuck in, but she too was snoring on the bed. I decided to sleep for a bit before the inevitable late night hassle. I reached up to turn the light off and sat down in the brown velvet chair under the window. Despite the quiet I couldn't sleep and I got to thinking about things again.

Bramble was over twenty years old by now and she wouldn't last forever. I'd miss her when she'd gone. Along with Floyd she had been a constant presence in my life, when often I couldn't rely on my family. I tended to be the odd one out when visiting my parents home. My brother lived at home until he was in his forties even after my mother had moved out alone into a flat of her own. My sister moved away to the coast after uni. and that left dad and my brother in dads house alone. Sometimes the family would go out for days together in my brothers car. I was never invited as David and I didn't get on. I felt David had pushed mum out of her home and that he should go and find somewhere of his own.

Without the support of a close family I tended to prefer the company of the animals in my care. Chris was mostly around to share space with and so things jogged along. The time at Ashleigh terrace was excruciatingly hard though and both Chris and I were feeling the strain. I was fed up with the town by now. Even after we'd moved to Chilton street things hadn't much improved. I decided to rent a house on the Somerset levels. It would be smaller than Bridgwater with its plethora of drunks and the dogs would have more fun in the country. Taking my courage in both hands I moved to a small town a few miles from Glastonbury. I rented a tiny cottage in a back lane perched up a precarious stone path. It was tall and narrow and belonged to a landlady who was living in India. The rent was cheap and the house was cold. It had an aga that didn't work and so I had to use a calor gas again. None of the rooms had any heating. By then my grandfather, Harold Heritage, had died from an industrial disease and I had some of grandmother Edith's furniture. A bookcase and some spelter statues. I'd bought a beautiful piece of art deco glass, signed by someone called C. Alexander and named 'The Vine'. It had been found in France by an antique dealer. I've always had a passion for stained glass, and so even if the house was unheated and the bedroom was cold at least the room would look wonderful basking in the rainbow colours thrown out from the leaded window. A friend lugged suitcases of my books up the narrow stairs to the front of the house and deposited them in my bedroom. I'd decided if I could heat one room it might as well be there. Floyd could curl up in the small space with me, and apart from the kitchen and bathroom there was only one more room which I decided to ignore. The tiny cottage should be cheap to keep and so without Chris I settled in there.

Chris had decided he wanted to be a father, although he didn't want a wife or female partner. So he'd gone in search of children to care for. He'd moved to Wales for a while and made friends with a couple of women who had children. They enjoyed communal life and would let him share childcare. The commune he moved into was run by vegans and would be inexpensive to live in. They chopped up pallets to fuel an open fire and searched for their food in skips outside supermarkets. While none of them ate meat they would pick it up from skips and sell it to villagers in the place they lived. That was then used to pay for water bills and sundries. The small Welsh village they lived in wasn't used to these characters and the locals from the working mens club unkindly called them soap dodgers.

The new cottage and routine was hard to get used to for me because someone important was missing. Chris had taken Bramble! Just around the time I had moved Chris and I had rowed and he'd stormed off with her while I was in the toilet. When I came out to find her my dear old friend was gone. I was bereft without her and concerned about her care. For a few months I was without her. Eventually Chris returned her to me. She was bloated and fat. Chris said he had kept her vegan but had fed her lots of bread culled from skips. As soon as I had her back I stuck on a pan of wholegrain rice with t.v.p. and lentils and lots of vegetables to simmer. She wolfed it down like a dog who had been starved, because her temporary diet with Chris probably hadn't had many nutrients in. With Bramble back I had a brief period of relief from worry. Then another bombshell dropped. My landlady returned from India and told me she wanted me to share the house with some biker friends of hers. She wanted to divide up the tiny cottage into some sort of micro house share. With so few rooms I did not think it was possible and anyway it was my home and I didn't want to share with unknown men.

When Chris was away I'd found another vegan man to hang out with. His name was Reg. He was a northerner who had come to the south west via a probation hostel where he claimed he'd been sent after fighting over money. This proved not to be the case but at the time I didn't know. Reg lived in Bridgwater and would visit me using the tatty moped Chris had left when he set off for his new life in the rubbish skips of Wales. Reg knew a bit about mechanics and by then I had an 'A' series Ford lorry that I was driving. A friend had sold it for a song after turning it into an enormous red living space. About the time the landlady had decided to try to move the bikers in I'd decided to sell the lorry. I advertised it in a vehicle mag. One morning when Reg was out in the lane showing it to someone who claimed to be a prospective buyer the landlady arrived mob handed with a group of her friends and came into the cottage through the door Reg had left open.
I came out of the kitchen with a cup of tea in my hand to find her at the bottom of the stairs with a crowd of people I didn't know. She said "I'm throwing you out, you're leaving today". My heart missed a beat and I couldn't speak for a second as I looked around at the mob that had entered my home. It was the worst moment in my life, bar losing Bramble, for a very long time. "You can't just evict me" I told her "I pay you rent, there are laws to protect me from this". She said "Get all her stuff out" to some traveller type men behind her. They started to go through my rooms bringing all my personal belongings out and piling them on the floor. Someone had picked up my fragile stained glass window and shoved it into

the hall. My Grandmothers bookcase was manhandled and bumped down the stairs.

Reg was still outside in the lorry and didn't hear me shout him to come in. About eleven people were picking up my stuff now and they began just throwing it out onto the steps in front of the cottage. Next someone started to hassle the dogs. By then Floyd and Bramble were being kept separately. Bramble had started to bully Floyd and so I didn't leave them together. Someone grabbed Floyd and thrust her outside of the door. They then went to try to get Bramble. This was causing the dogs extreme stress and I asked the crowd not to shove the dogs together because I thought it would cause them to fight. Just as my large landlady was about to grab Bramble and shove her down the stairs a policeman arrived. Reg had come out of the lorry, seen what was happening and dialled 999. Floyd was still sat bewildered on the front steps and Bramble was fizzing with supressed annoyance. A huge sigh of relief moved through my body as the policeman ushered everyone out. He spoke to the landlady and myself. He said she claimed I was happy to have a hand moving out. I told him she was lying. The crowd were moved on and Reg fixed a new bolt on the door. The cottage was a mess with all my stuff piled in the hall. Some of my things were broken.

When Reg went outside to check on my car it was gone, he said the landladies friends must have taken it. After that incident I stayed in the cottage a few more days, but didn't feel safe. I sold my stained glass to my antique dealer brother for a pittance to sell on and with the money I put diesel in the lorry and moved out of my home. This incident left a really bad taste in my mouth, and when I think of this small town I can never help remembering the film Straw Dogs, because that's what it felt like to live there for those last few days. Sitting in the dark at Wellington road with Bramble, Sally and Stan I had the benefit of hindsight and bad though that episode was I'd had no idea things were about to get much, much worse.

After the landlady debacle Bramble, Floyd and I moved into my lorry. The seven and a half tonner had been turned into a living van by a friend at the time called Mel. Mel lived in a van in a conifer plantation. He didn't like houses and lived outdoors with his dogs. He'd been doing up the 'A' series I bought from him and had put a door in the side, installed a wood burning stove and even a tiny stained glass window. With the cottage gone I had to live in the lorry. Reg piled all my stuff into it for me, which my father then let me store in his house, albeit unwillingly. I put a container for logs in, some cutlery, crockery and my sleeping bags, and Reg hauled in the dog baskets; Floyds beloved whicker bed full of her precious tennis balls and Brambles comfy blue plastic dog bed. Reg was living in a house in Bridgwater and needed to get home early. So my first night as a homeless person, and in fact every other, was spent with my dogs alone. I wasn't sure where it would be safe to park and I didn't want to get attacked so I drove the dogs up to a parking spot near Wind down. It was quite ironic to think that when Chris and I had the bailiffs come round at Ashleigh terrace that I'd thought things couldn't get any worse. Now here we were with no fixed abode in a tatty lorry. As I had no home I couldn't get a job, and I had to keep asking my dad if I could use his house for a bath. I asked if we could move into his four bedroomed house with him as he was at that point living there alone as David had briefly moved out, but dad didn't like dogs and I refused to part from them so the smokey lorry had to become our temporary home.

For about a year Floyd, Bramble and I slept and ate in the lorry. In the summer we could stay on the canal path where we would be left alone to spend the day. When you have nothing you cannot participate in society. Any money I acquired had to be spent on food or fuel for the lorry. Also, as it was old, it would never start in the morning and had to be jump started by a taxi each day. I became adept at finding quiet spots to park in, mostly laybys. Usually I would park near other lorries. Bramble would sleep on the seats in the cab and bark loudly if she spotted any trouble.

General election time approached and I wanted to vote for whoever would understand about poverty and homelessness. In my naiveté I assumed someone would, but homeless people could not vote so the election passed me by.

I took to visiting the local Art centre in the evenings so I could keep warm. The stove in the van was all smoke and no heat. One of the older men I knew from the Arts centre invited me round to his house for a glass of wine. We shared a love of eastern poetry and I felt quite safe in his home. After a while he offered me a bed in the back room of his house but the dogs had to stay in the van. I was very uneasy about leaving them although they were only one street away. Later the guy allowed me to move them in after some horrible teenagers kept banging on the side of the lorry. Then the lorry broke down. We were now homeless properly and entirely dependant on the goodwill of my poetry loving friend. After another few months of horror and hassle Chris returned to the town. He was looking for someone to share a house with. When he saw the precariousness of the life of the dogs and I we sat and had a long talk. Things had not gone well for him in the commune. He hated looking for food in skips and found the other residents hard to talk to. He had spent most of his time in his room. Hardly the wildest of adventures. The women had used him as a baby sitting service, which he didn't mind, but really he just felt on the edge of things. He'd already given Bramble back to me so had just been on his own. He had come back to town and wanted to talk to his old friend.

At last there was the possibility of sharing a house again. I could find a job and the dogs would be safe. I decided I never wanted to be in such a dangerous position again. I had never had the chance to finish my education whilst working in low paid jobs and I felt like I wanted to go back to learning. With Chris back around to share some bills I decided to try to get to university.

Bramble and Floyd were delighted to get back to the routine of a fixed abode. Whilst we were homeless I had managed to keep them fed, sheltered and safe, but it was a huge relief to be able to go behind a front door and bolt it shut. Not to be moved on by the police. Not to have to worry about every unfamiliar noise at night. I got to sleep in a bed again instead of the cab overhang in the lorry. Luxury at last. These were my last thoughts as I fell asleep in the brown chair under the window in Wellington road with the dogs.

Life at Wellington road established a regular pattern. I got a place at college and did an access course. This led to a place at university. By then Floyd was older and was soon to die. After I lost her we took on Sally and she became a companion for ageing Bramble. By now Bramble was making records with her age. She started to become known as the worlds oldest bitch. Photographers from national newspapers came to take her picture, and magazines did stories on her while she basked in the limelight. She was becoming geriatric, and began to need more care from me. We stuck to her routines and life became a gentle amble down the river for her with Chris while I studied English at U.W.E. in Bristol. I was also working full time as an activities coordinator now and life was very full on.

Sally and Bramble got on fine, although Sally could be a little assertive. Once or twice we saw her push Bramble off her bed. Sally had started to bite her tail and I took her to the vet to be looked at. He advised different flea control and soothing homeopathic tablets. Still she carried on biting. She had begun to slow up whilst walking and I began to wonder if she had cancer. The vet thought not, as her appetite was good and her weight stable. After a while she began to cry out while biting and we went back to the vet a few more times. Eventually cancer was diagnosed and we decided for her sake the vet must put her down. Sally's last walk with Bramble and I was at Kingscliffe, near North Petherton. It was a tract of land full of chestnut trees, streams and wild flowers. At certain times of year there are baby frogs in puddles and myriad squirrels chase through the trees. There is so much pleasure there for dogs. On our last trip there we didn't really walk much. Sally pottered around slowly and Bramble stayed by her side. After a few minutes we sat back in the car and watched the scene from there. It had been bright but it started to drizzle with rain. Sat between my two elderly dogs, one of whom was about to die, I felt very sad indeed. I stroked Sally's back and told her how much I loved her. I said she had been a very kind friend and I thanked her for her company. Tears coursed down my cheeks because the next day she had been booked in at the vets to die. Sally, who had been accepting comfort from me sat up and looked into my eyes. She put a paw on my arm and then reached up and licked the tears off my face. I think she was acknowledging my sadness at her imminent departure. I looked up at the sky and to the right of us was a rainbow arching near white clouds. I read it as a sign for the future. At this late in the day Chris had said he wasn't up to taking on anymore dogs, and Bramble was old in the extreme. I knew that soon it might be the last time I ever looked after a dog. I comforted myself with the fact I would have friends with dogs and they would always be in my life. Slowly and carefully I drove the 'old ladies' as Chris and I referred to Sally and Bramble, home.

Sally slept a lot and I felt an aching sadness. The next day she was still tired and we knew the cancer would not get better. The vet had not advised us to operate and it was time to put Sally down. Chris and I drove to Taunton without speaking, except to reassure Sally that soon any stress would be over. Before the deed was done we took a last few photos of our friend and we knelt down and kissed her goodbye. We had asked the vet to euthenase her in the car because we wanted her to die somewhere familiar. At the last minute the surgery seemed too stark and clinical to say goodbye to our dear friend. The vet put a needle into Sally and the drug was directed into her. She jumped and tried to pull her paw away, looking up at me in fear, "It's okay Sally" I told her, at which point her body went limp and she died. Her last view of the world was of the people who loved her trying to take her fear away. Chris said on his last walk in the park with her she had reached up to him and kissed his eyes. He believed she was thanking him for putting in her eye drops every day, to stop her eyes going dry.

Chris and I took Sally's body home so we could show Bramble that she was dead before we put her in the freezer. I hoped one day to buy a little plot of land where I could bury my beautiful canine friends together. Chris lay Sally gently on her bed on a blanket and Bramble got up from her own bed to see what had happened to Sally. Sally looked the same as ever but no doubt had the chemical smells of death that dogs can read. Bramble sniffed along the length of Sally's body and appeared to understand that her friend had died. Chris and I stroked Sally's back for a few minutes leaving her with Bramble for half an hour so she could say goodbye. Then Chris gently picked Sally up and Bramble followed us into the kitchen where he put her into the freezer with Floyd. We told Bramble "One day the dogs will be put in a garden under the grass and they will stay there forever". Bramble paused for a few seconds then ambled back to her room to lay back on her bed.

The loss of Sally was a big blow for Bramble. By then all our other dogs had died. Sally was Brambles last canine friend. Although at first Bramble seemed to accept Sally's death, a few days later she began to pace her room. She walked round and round the edge just like she had done in my garden the first day I had brought her home. She seemed very anxious. Chris and I took her to the vet who diagnosed cancer. At twenty five years old an operation was out of the question, the anasthetic would probably kill her and even if it didn't, trying to recover would sap her strength. The vet said he didn't think she was in any pain at that point but was missing Sally.

After the vets we went walking with her, then fed her and settled her down. Afterwards it was time to sit and think about the implications of what the vet had said. We were going to lose Bramble and have to put her down.

I had the most appalling sinking feeling in my stomach, by now familiar to me having recently lost Sally. I sat on the edge of a chair and tried to concentrate on my breathing. Bramble had been with me longer than Floyd was. We had shared our entire lives together for so many years. Finding it hard to contemplate the death of another dog only two weeks after Sally died I went up to bed and gave way to oblivion.

The next day at dog walking time I couldn't decide where to take Bramble. Maybe we should stick to St. Mathews field or the park. Somewhere close in case she got poorly. On the other hand Bramble hadn't visited the beach for a while and she might not get another chance. Chris and I decided to take her to Burnham on sea, ten miles down the road from home and we gently lifted her into my car.

At Burnham we stayed on the beach for some time. It was a warm day and quite still, no sand blew in our faces and breeze gently ruffled our hair. The sea had come in, wetting the sand and leaving a few shells around. There was a piece of cuttlefish washed up which Bramble sniffed. She walked slowly around looking at what I think was her favourite place. Perhaps she was remembering all the times she had chased the waves and barked at them with Stan. Or maybe she was remembering running along with Floyd on a windy day when she was a wild, frightened youngster, or more sedate walks with Sally, who liked to drag a big stick along. Or maybe she was remembering Chris and I, one of us always with her, day in day out for twenty five years.

Whatever she was thinking she came over to me and stood by my side. She seemed tired. I put my arms around her and we looked out towards the sea. The sun had begun to set and the tide was starting to drift back in, swirling waves were edging towards us. I picked Bramble up in my arms with some difficulty, my back was stiff and painful. Like her I was no longer young. I held her to me. She felt light as a feather, very different to the muscled young lady who had climbed trees with Floyd.

I knew that she would be dead soon and I wanted to communicate something to her. Some idea that everything and everyone goes on after death in some sort of way. That this part of her life was safe for her to enter because it is part of a circle. I stood with her in my arms with the tide washing up to my feet. The sky was red and pink over the sea. A fierce sunset began to unfold, "Look" I told her "The earth is saying goodbye to Bramble"

Chris came over to us and gently took Bramble in his arms. I walked back away from them a little so they could say a private goodbye. The tide was coming up to them, then edging away, then rushing back again. Chris bent his head to Brambles ear to whisper something to her. I don't know what he said.

Before it began to get cold we started to walk back towards the car. Chris went slightly ahead carrying the tired old lady. As he ascended the slope from the beach she turned round to look back behind her for one last time, at her favourite place. She knew she would never be there again.

We put Bramble into the car. It seemed like the time had come to say goodbye. She was quiet now and somehow I felt her drifting away from us. We drove her to her vet in Taunton and asked him to put her down. Alistair lay Bramble on the table in his consulting room where she'd been several times before. We didn't want her to be frightened and we asked if he could give her an anesthetic to put her out before he did the deed. The vet gave her an injection then left the room to give us time to say goodbye. Bramble closed her eyes, and made a small sound in her throat, I stroked her and told her I loved her, that everything that was happening was how it should be. I told her she was going to sleep forever and we would not see each other again. I remembered how a week ago she had come up to me in the car and put her paw on my arm to pull me closer to her, a last hug from my fierce friend. Now the old dog on the table was off on her final adventure. Alistair came back in and put the lethal drug into Brambles vein. Her eyes dilated and then she was gone. The oldest Bitch in the world and more importantly my staunchest friend had died.

Chris and I drove Bramble home in the back seat of my car. She would be an impossible act to follow. We tried to think of a fitting tribute for her and we came up with this; Bramble was the dog who wanted to live forever, and in terms of dog years, she did.

Brambles says goodbye to the beach

Printed in Great Britain
by Amazon